Boethius

THE POEMS FROM

ON THE CONSOLATION OF PHILOSOPHY

TRANSLATED OUT OF THE ORIGINAL LATIN

INTO DIVERSE HISTORICAL ENGLISHINGS

DILIGENTLY COLLAGED BY

Peter Glassgold

LOS ANGELES

SUN & MOON PRESS

1994

Sun & Moon Press
A Program of The Contemporary Arts Educational Project, Inc.
a nonprofit corporation
6026 Wilshire Boulevard, Los Angeles, California 90036

This edition first published in paperback in 1994 by Sun & Moon Press
10 9 8 7 6 5 4 3 2 1
FIRST EDITION
© 1990, 1994 by Peter Glassgold
Portions of this book were first published in *Washington Review*.
The epigraph on page 9 is from Primo Levi's *Survival in Auschwitz*, translated by Stuart Woolf
(New York: Macmillan Publishing Company), © 1959 by The Orion Press.
The epigraph on page 17 is from Edward Sapir's *Language*,
© 1921 by Harcourt, Brace & World, copyright renewed © 1949 by Jean V. Sapir.
Quotations from Edward Gibbon's *The Decline and Fall of the Roman Empire*
on pp. 13 and 173 are from The Modern Library edition, ed. Oliphant Smeaton
(New York: Random House, n.d.) All rights reserved

This book was made possible, in part, through an operational grant from the
Andrew W. Mellon Foundation, through a production grant from
the National Endowment for the Arts and through contributions to
The Contemporary Arts Educational Project, Inc.,
a nonprofit corporation

Cover: Paul Klee, *Open Book*, 1930
Reprinted by permission of the Solomon R. Guggenheim Museum
Cover Design: Katie Messborn
Typography: Guy Bennett

LIBRARY OF CONGRESS CATALOGING IN PUBLISHING DATA
Glassgold, Peter
Boethius: The Poems from
On the Consolation of Philosophy
Translated Out of the Original Latin
into Diverse Historical Englishings
Diligently Collaged
ISBN: 1-55713-109-0
I. Title. II. Series.
811'.54—dc20

Printed in the United States of America on acid-free paper.

For Suzanne
for Jack
for Douglas

CONTENTS

"Imagine now a man who is deprived of everyone he loves, and at the same time of his house, his habits, his clothes, in short, of everything he possessed: he will be a hollow man, reduced to suffering and needs, forgetful of dignity and restraint, for he who loses all often easily loses himself."

—PRIMO LEVI

Foreword

THE NAME Boethius is scarcely recognized nowadays beyond academic circles where Latin is still read. Yet from his death in 524 A.D. and onward into the nineteenth century, he was held along with Socrates—and in the course of time, Thomas à Beckett and Thomas More—as a consummate martyr of conscience, a man of intellect and influence who, fallen from political grace, could rise above his personal agony to an impersonal magnanimity that shamed his murderers by its example. Boethius, however, had no Plato to immortalize him, turning his life and pedagogy into essential world drama. And though, like Beckett and More, he was eventually canonized by the Church, his vocation did not straddle the collective historical inheritance of the English-speaking world; the northern Italian cult of St. Severinus Boethius is strictly local.

He was born in Rome around 480, at an historical cusp. Italy had fallen to its Germanic conquerors in 476 but still retained the trappings of Roman independence. Anicius Manlius Severinus Boethius came from a well-connected, aristocratic family that had produced two emperors and would produce one pope, Gregory the Great. Orphaned as a boy, he was brought up in and married into the household of Quintus Aurelius Symmachus, whose great-grandfather of the same name (a friend of the poet Ausonius) had fought vainly against the Christian abolition of traditional pagan public ceremony. Boethius himself was raised as an orthodox Catholic during the long reign of Theodoric, the heterodox Arian king of the Ostrogoths, but was thoroughly educated in the classics and philosophy and may even have studied at the Platonic Academy in Athens (which was to be closed permanently on religious grounds by Emperor Justinian in 529).

As a philosopher, Boethius' unachieved aim was to translate into Latin all of Plato and Aristotle, making his own synthesizing commentaries. He wrote on mathematics, music, and theology. As a public man, Boethius fared well under Theodoric. He became consul in 510—as his father and father-in-law had been before him—and saw his two sons in a double consulship in 522, the year he himself was appointed to the ministry of master of offices, which controlled the civil service. But his outspoken character made him a pawn in the rival intrigues between Roman and Goth, Catholic and Arian, and, inevitably, Theodoric and the emperor in Constantinople. In 524,

Boethius was accused of treason, stripped of his rank and honors, tried *in absentia*, and condemned to death. Exiled to Pavia in the north, imprisoned and in chains, he wrote his *On the Consolation of Philosophy* (*De Consolatione Philosophiae*), which Gibbon called "a golden volume not unworthy of the leisure of Plato or Tully, but which claims incomparable merit from the barbarism of the times and the situation of the author."

On the Consolation of Philosophy is divided into five short "books," each consisting of alternate sections of whole poems and prose dialogues between Boethius and the goddess Philosophy, concerning humanity's evident helplessness in the face of fate and fortune. Boethius' Latin has antique, classical polish, and the poems themselves are written for the most part in traditional quantitative meters. But it was not so much style as sentiment that drew later readers to Boethius' meditative sorrows and the fact that until the Renaissance, the *Consolation* was one of the few books to carry on intact Neoplatonic philosophical discourse. Its influence was especially strong in English, a language whose literature and development has been bound to translation almost from the start. Alfred the Great, England's first literary translator, made a prose translation of it and may have been the author of the Old English alliterative versions of the poems. Chaucer, too, translated the *Consolation* into prose, and his later work—principally *The Canterbury Tales* and *Troilus and Criseyde*—shows an unmistakably Boethian cast. In 1593, Elizabeth I, in an access of royal frenzy, made a wonderfully raw translation into poetry and prose in the course of less than a month and in no more than twenty-seven hours. These three are not the only ones to have turned the *Consolation* into English, but they throw an awesome shadow, and not the least because of their own hard experience of the tenuousness and arbitrariness of autocratic power. Gibbon notes that Boethius' work gains in honor by Alfred's attention to it—and one should add by extension, Chaucer's and Elizabeth's as well. Gibbon's aside anticipates the modern view of translation, expressed by Walter Benjamin, that sees it as part of the "afterlife" of a literary work, in which the original attains an "ever-renewed and most abundant flowering."

In producing a new translation of a previously translated classic, what practical use is made of the flowerings of yesteryear? Generally, very little. The expressive capabilities of any language naturally shift over the centuries, and though one might envy the rhetorical range of another era, it is appropriated largely for archaizing effect: the underlying purpose of translation is most commonly to re-create the original in the language of one's own time. Thus due respect is paid to the efforts of translators of the historical past. It is the more nearly contemporaneous versions one must respond to, however silently: translator A's choice of words will, perforce, impinge upon the choice of translator B twenty or thirty years later.

Some literary works, however, seem to gain not just

in honor but complexity from the many translations made of them. Boethius' *Consolation* is such a text, and in making the present versions of the poems, I have allowed historical resonance full play. Alfred, Chaucer, Elizabeth, and their contemporaries have given me entrée into the language of their own times. I have drawn freely from this music, composing phrases or whole lines in mixed varieties of English, borrowing words if need be from the translators of earlier eras. I have kept most ancient spellings as I found them, as visual counterparts to the translations' historical—or in linguistic terms, diachronic— sound-collage. The prose dialogues have been retained in summary, as a dramatic framework for the poetry's philosophical lyricism, which seeks in translation a language transcending time, echoing and reechoing Boethius' dream of the eternal ideal.

Peter Glassgold

"All grammars leak."

—EDWARD SAPIR

A Note on Texts, Method, and Pronunciation

THE TRANSLATIONS in this book are based upon the Latin texts established in The Loeb Classical Library edition of: *Boethius: The Theological Tractates and The Consolation of Philosophy*, edited and translated by E.K. Rand and H.F. Stewart (1918); revised by S.J. Tester (1973). Cambridge, Massachusetts: Harvard University Press, 1973.

Several early English versions of Boethius were consulted regularly.

King Alfred's Anglo-Saxon Version of Boethius, De Consolatione Philosophiae, edited and translated by Samuel Fox. London: Bohn's Antiquarian Library, 1864; reprinted, New York: AMS Press, 1970. This edition prints the Old English texts in a type version of medieval Anglo-Saxon semiuncials rather than transliterating them into the modern alphabet. The volume also includes the alliterative *Metres of Boethius*, along with a poor translation into variously rhyming verses by Martin F. Tupper, "ESQ., D.C.L., &c., &c., &c."

The Paris Psalter and The Meters of Boethius, edited by
George Philip Krapp. The Anglo-Saxon Poetic Records,
volume V. New York: Columbia University Press, 1932.

*Chaucer's Translation of Boethius' "De Consolatione
Philosophiae,"* edited by Richard Morris. The Early En-
glish Text Society, Extra Series, No. 5. London: Oxford
University Press, 1868. This edition reproduces
uncorrected British Museum Additional Ms. 10,340, col-
lated with Cambridge University Library Ms. Ii:3.21. A
regularized version of "Boece," prepared by Ralph Hanna
III and Traugott Lawler, is provided in *The Riverside Chau-
cer*, 3rd Edition, Larry D. Benson, general editor. Boston:
Houghton Mifflin, 1987.

*Boethius: De Consolatione Philosophiae, Translated by John
Walton*, edited by Mark Science. The Early English Text
Society, Original Series, No. 170. London: Oxford Uni-
versity Press, 1927; reprinted, Millwood, N.Y.: Kraus
Reprint, 1975. John Walton, Canon of Osney, was com-
missioned to make his translation by Elizabeth Berkeley,
Countess of Warwick. Completed in 1410, Walton's
work derives directly from Chaucer and is cast entirely in
rhyming seven-line stanzas patterned after *Troilus and
Criseyde*.

*Queen Elizabeth's Englishings of Boethius, Plutarch and
Horace*, edited by Caroline Pemberton. The Early English
Text Society, Original Series, No. 113. London: Kegan
Paul, Trench, Trubner & Co., 1899; reprinted, Millwood,
N.Y.: Kraus Reprint, 1975. An appendix includes the

rhyming translations made by Sir Thomas Challoner in 1663 of poems in Books I and II.

My approach to these various texts evolved from the patascholarship of my "back" translations of American modernist poems into Old English (*Hwæt!*, 1985), in which I tested two constructs of linguistic "purity" (the historical and the modernist aesthetic) on the critical grid of translation. Then as now, by putting new demands on the resources of early English, I have wrung something fresh—and I think beautiful—from the supposedly "dead" ancestral strains of our language. I have called these translations sound-collages, indicating that they fall outside the bounds of conventional grammar; but like any macaronic composition, they have an essential logic: in this case, of historical English. However, because they range through so many layers of the language—with many words keeping the same form, or nearly so, throughout— pronunciation can only be approximate. And in fact, the tension between the visual and oral response to antique spellings reflects a natural uncertainty: no language remains fixed.

I respect the essential integrity of Boethius' line. He is not a poet of great complexity, but when his lines end-stop or run on, mine generally stop or run with them. Some of the translations mirror, however distantly, the metrical formalities of his quantitative Latin verses, in either syllabics or loose accents. Thus:

Two-stress line (with an extra stress in the final line): I,7.

Eight syllables: ii,8; iii,12; iv,3.

Nine syllables: iii,1 (in the English only); iv,6 (with ten syllables in a full-stop line); v,2.

Couplets: of alternate eleven and ten syllables, iii,4; with syllabic shortening of alternate lines, iii,5; alternate four-and three-stress, iii,8; alternate five- and six-stress, v,1; alternate five- and four-stress, iv,5.

Three-stress line: iii,7 (with an extra stress in the final line); v,4.

Eleven syllables: iv,7.

Five-stress line: iii,11.

Six-stress line: v,5.

iii,6 rhymes internally, at the caesura and line's end. In the Latin original, there is a clear midline pause but no rhyme, which is not an element of classical poetry. In Boethius' verses, end-rhymes apparent to the English-speakers' eye and ear are in fact functions of an internal assonantal and alliterative pattern; in my translations, they are serendipitous materials in the sound-collage.

For the phonetic values of Old English and Middle English letters, Latin is the best general guide, with a few exceptions.

In this book, the runic "thorn" (Þ,þ) represents the Old English "th" combination, often used in Middle English as well. Þ is voiced (as in "rather") between vowels and between a vowel and another voiced consonant. It is unvoiced ("thin") in all other positions and when doubled.

The letters *f* and *v* follow the same voiced and unvoiced pattern (as in modern *v* and *z*).

The *æ* ligature in Old English is pronounced pl*ay* as a long vowel and th*at* when short.

The letters c and g in Old English have both a hard (*k*, *g*) and soft (*ch*, *y*) sound. The soft manner is printed here as *ċ* and *ġ*. The combination cg is voiced c (as in "fu*dge*"). *Sċ* is generally pronounced in a soft manner ("*sh*ip").

In Old English, *h* initially or in combination (*hw*, *hl*, *hr*) is always pronounced, and with the modern breathing sound. Otherwise, it is gutturalized, as in German or Scots; Middle English sometimes substitutes *gh*.

P G

Liber 1 / Book 1

I

Carmina qui quondam studio florente peregi,
     Flebilis heu maestos cogor inire modos.
Ecce mihi lacerae dictant scribenda camenae
     Et veris elegi fletibus ora rigant.
Has saltem nullus potuit pervincere terror,
     Ne nostrum comites prosequerentur iter.
Gloria felicis olim viridisque iuventae
     Solantur maesti nunc mea fata senis.
Venit enim properata malis inopina senectus
     et dolor aetatem iussit inesse suam.
Intempestivi funduntur vertice cani
     et tremit effeto corpore laxa cutis.
Mors hominum felix quae se nec dulcibus annis

[A.D. 524. *A prison tower in Pavia in the north of Italy. An-icius Manlius Severinus Boethius, ex-consul, former minister and confidant of Theodoric, the Ostrogothic king of Rome, sits in chains. A victim of court intrigue, he has been accused of treasonous correspondence with the Emperor Justin in Constantinople and summarily exiled, banished from home and family and even the solace of his library. Grieving and old before his time, Boethius now looks to the Muses for comfort.*]

I

Hwæt, iċ hwilum ġedyde songez in florysching studie,
    sorgleoþ la! I wepyng am cumpeld to begin.
Me the muses rent dictate I must write,
    and elegies wiþ verray teers my face bedew.
No terror at þe leest þo muses mihte ofercuman
    that they ne beon fellow travelers following my way.
The one-time glory of happy griny youthe
    now relieves the fate of me olde man sorgfull.
For elde is comen unlookt for hied by harmes
    and sar haþ hoten his age to add withal.
Hoore herys untimely ar powrd upon my hed
    and from a weakened corse the loose skin quivers.
Happy the death of men that in the switest years intrudes

Inserit et maestis saepe vocata venit.
Eheu quam surda miseros avertitur aure
Et flentes oculos claudere saeva negat.
Dum levibus male fida bonis fortuna faveret,
Paene caput tristis merserat hora meum.
Nunc quia fallacem mutavit nubila vultum,
Protrahit ingratas impia vita moras.
Quid me felicem totiens iactastis amici?
Qui cecidit, stabili non erat ille gradu.

not but comeþ in sorwynges often called.
Eala! wiþ how deef an eere sche fro wrecches wries
    and cruel refraines from closing weeping eyes.
While Fortune untriewu favored me with vading goodz
    death's sad hour hadde almost dreynt myne heued.
Now since Fortune cloudy haþ chaunged her fikle face,
    pitiless life drags on unkyndely its delays.
Why me so oft, my frendz! did you boaste a happie man?
    Se feoll, næs his stæpe næfre fæst.

II

Heu quam praecipiti mersa profundo
Mens hebet et propria luce relicta
Tendit in externas ire tenebras,
Terrenis quotiens flatibus aucta
Crescit in inmensum noxia cura.
Hic quondam caelo liber aperto
Suetus in aetherios ire meatus
Cernebat rosei lumina solis,
Visebat gelidae sidera lunae
Et quaecumque vagos stella recursus
Exercet varios flexa per orbes,
Comprensam numeris victor habebat.
Quin etiam causas unde sonora

[The goddess Philosophy appears and drives away the Muses,
"those stagey little whores"; their dulcet poison can only palli-
ate the anguish of a man such as Boethius, nurtured on the
ancient philosophers. She laments his mind's distress:]

II

Eala! how in ouerþrowyng depnesse the drowned
mind is dull and forlete by its own light
tends to move in to foreyne derknesses,
ofte swoln wiþ worldly wyndes
grows immense from noyous cure.
This man once free under the open sky
wont to gone on aery paþes
would scan the rays of þe rosene sunne,
regard the cold moon's constellations,
and what star elz wandryng recourses
runs yflit thro divers spheres
he held grasp of, þe maistrie by noumbre.
Yea eke þe causes whennes sounyg

Flamina sollicitent aequora ponti,
Quis volvat stabilem spiritus orbem
Vel cur hesperias sidus in undas
Casurum rutilo surgat ab ortu,
Quid veris placidas temperet horas,
Ut terram roseis floribus ornet,
Quis dedit ut pleno fertilis anno
Autumnus gravidis influat uvis
Rimari solitus atque latentis
Naturae varias reddere causas,
Nunc iacet effeto lumine mentis
Et pressus gravibus colla catenis
Declivemque gerens pondere vultum
Cogitur, heu, stolidam cernere terram.

gusts roil the surface of the sea;
hwelċ gast tyrneþ þa fæste worulde
or whie the welkyn in þe westren wawes
yfalle rises in the ruddy east;
what tempers springtime's lusty houres
that erthe be deckt with rosy floures;
who makes autumn in the fullness of the year
fleten in fertile with heavy grapes—
these he used to probe and also hidden
nature's sondry causes to explain.
Now he lies of mindz light weakened
and nekke pressid by overheuy chaines,
his chere holding downcast for the weighte,
cumpeld, eala! to scan the dreary earth.

III

Tunc me discussa liquerunt nocte tenebrae
      Luminibusque prior rediit vigor,
Ut, cum praecipiti glomerantur sidera Coro
      Nimbosisque polus stetit imbribus,
Sol latet ac nondum caelo venientibus astris,
      Desuper in terram nox funditur;
Hanc si Threicio Boreas emissus ab antro
      Verberet et clausam reseret diem,
Emicat ac subito vibratus lumine Phoebus
      Mirantes oculos radiis ferit.

[*"But time now for healing," she says, "not complaint." Bo-
ethius, stupefied, can hardly recognize the goddess he had for-
merly known so well. She touches him and with a tuck of her
dress wipes away his tears, clearing his blurry eyes for a mo-
ment of the cloud of mortal cares.*]

III

Then with night toshake the darknesses were clear
        and to myn eyen repeyre ageyne hiera ærran mæġen:
as when the heavens amass in a headlong nor'wester
        and the sky is thick wiþ wet ploungy cloudes,
the sun lies hid, no stars yet moeuyng in þe firmament,
        a night ufan on earth is spread—
if Boreas loosed from his Thracian den
        dothe strike and descouereþ þe closed day,
flashes out Phoebus vibrant with light, sudden
        radiances piercing astonied eyen.

IV

Quisquis composito serenus aevo
Fatum sub pedibus egit superbum
Fortunamque tuens utramque rectus
Invictum potuit tenere vultum,
Non illum rabies minaeque ponti
Versum funditus exagitantis aestum
Nec ruptis quotiens vagus caminis
Torquet fumificos Vesaevus ignes
Aut celsas soliti ferire turres
Ardentis via fulminis movebit.
Quid tantum miseri saevos tyrannos
Mirantur sine viribus furentes?
Nec speres aliquid nec extimescas,

[*Boethius remembers the goddess Philosophy's face and won-*
ders at her presence in his cell. "Would I," she asks, "abandon
my protégé, desert him on the lonely road?" This is not the first
time an innocent man has been condemned for her sake; wis-
dom has always been a goad to ignorant rage. But though the
ranks of stupidity besiege us, we can look down at them and
laugh; they can never reach our heights.]

IV

Who serene in settled life
haþ put proud fate underfote
and rihtwis eyeing eyþer fortune
may holde his chere unwon:
neither rage and menace of the sea
uphurling flodwielm fro þe botme;
ne swa oft of forborstenum ofnum wod
Vesuvius uncoils its smoking fires;
nor bolt lightning's path wont to smyte
heye toures—noght schal not moeue him.
Wherto þen wrecches do they wonder
at fiers tirants, forsles, frenzied?
Ne wene þu nawihtes ne ondræde,

Exarmaveris impotentis iram.
At quisquis trepidus pavet vel optat,
Quod non sit stabilis suique iuris,
Abiecit clipeum locoque motus
Nectit qua valeat trahi catenam.

bewæpnaſt þæs unmæhtiġes ierre.
But whoso quakyng feares or wische,
nis not ſtable and of his owene ryght,
hath acaſt his shild and poſt abandoned
binds the chain that drags him.

V

O stelliferi conditor orbis
Qui perpetuo nixus solio
Rapido caelum turbine versas
Legemque pati sidera cogis,
Ut nunc pleno lucida cornu
Totis fratris obvia flammis
Condat stellas luna minores,
Nunc obscuro pallida cornu
Phoebo proprior lumina perdat,
Et qui primae tempore noctis
Agit algentes Hesperos ortus,
Solitas iterum mutet habenas
Phoebi pallens Lucifer ortu.

["*Do you understand this,*" *she asks,* "*has it sunk into your mind?*" *Boethius responds by detailing his misfortunes. After a lifetime in Philosophy's service, in the cause of public justice, is this his reward? to be falsely accused, stripped of his books and everything he owns, all dignity and honor, tried and condemned without a chance to defend himself? Because of his downfall, innocent people are terrified, while corruption thrives. He must cry out:*]

V

La! shaper of the starry sphere
who set upon a lasting heahsetle
turnest þe heuene with hræþum sweye
and cumpelst the skies þi lawe to obeye:
that now the moon full hornèd
metyng all þe bemes hir broþer
bright dimmes the lesser stars,
then pale with horn obscure
nearra Phoebus loses her light,
and what at nightfall Hesperus hight,
þe euesterre, cold comes risen
exchangeth againe her wonted reynes:
Lucifer wans with Phoebus rising.

Tu frondifluae frigore brumae
Stringis lucem breviore mora:
Tu, cum fervida venerit aestas,
Agiles nocti dividis horas.
Tua vis varium temperat annum
Ut quas Boreae spiritus aufert
Revehat mites Zephyrus frondes
Quaeque Arcturus semina vidit
Sirius altas urat segetes.
Nihil antiqua lege solutum
Linquit propriae stationis opus.
Omnia certo fine gubernans
Hominum solos respuis actus
Merito rector cohibere modo.
Nam cur tantas lubrica versat
Fortuna vices? Premit insontes
Debita sceleri noxia poena,
At perversi resident celso
Mores solio sanctaque calcant
Iniusta vice colla nocentes.
Latet obscuris condita virtus
Clara tenebris iustusque tulit
Crimen iniqui.
Nil periuria, nil nocet ipsis
Fraus mendaci compta colore.
Sed cum libuit viribus uti,
Quos innumeri metuunt populi
Summos gaudent subdere reges.

Þu on winterċealde when leaves do fall
reſtreineſt dai liht to a briefer span:
þu þaþa sumorhæte is cumen
divideſt swifte þe tides of þe niht.
Þi miht attempreþ þe variaunt yere:
what Boreas' breath haþ reft awey
Zephyrus bringeþ agein, tender foliage,
while the seeds Arċturus saw
ben heye cornes when Sirius eschaufeþ hem.
Naught loused from auncient law
forleteþ the work of his propre eſtat.
All þing rewling with set purpose
only the deeds of men refoweſtow,
reċċere, to check in dewe mesure.
Forwhy does shifty Fortune so grete
entrechaunginges devise? oppress the innocent
with anoious peyne for the wicked meet,
but unrihtdæde sitten on heah-
setle and the guilty ofertredaþ
þe nekkes of holy men, injuſt requite.
In derkenesses ġehydd bright
virtue lies and þe rihtwise beriþ
þe felownes blame.
No perjury, no fraud harms
them kembd wiþ a fals colour.
But when hem lyſt to usen powre
heahcyningas whom countless people
dread they delight to underput.

O iam miseras respice terras
Quisquis rerum foedera nectis.
Operis tanti pars non vilis
Homines quatimur fortunae salo.
Rapidos rector comprime fluctus
Et quo caelum regis immensum
Firma stabiles foedere terras.

Nu la! look upon the wretched earth
whosoever knyttest the bondz of all:
of so grete a werke no mean a part
we men are tossed in the sea of fortune.
Represse, reċċere, the rushing floods
and wiþ þilke bonde þou rewlest heaven
wide maca staþolfæste þe erþe.

VI

Cum Phoebi radiis grave
Cancri sidus inaestuat,
Tum qui larga negantibus
Sulcis semina credidit,
Elusus Cereris fide
Quernas pergat ad arbores.
Numquam purpureum nemus
Lecturus violas petas
Cum saevis aquilonibus
Stridens campus inhorruit,
Nec quaeras avida manu
Vernos stringere palmites,
Uvis libeat frui;

[*Philosophy stays calm. "I hadn't realized," she says, "how remote is your exile and just how far you have driven yourself from your true homeland." What is missing from Boethius' cell is not his books so much as the ideas that she, Philosophy, had put in them. Boethius has accurately told the injustices done him (and been modest about his good accomplishments). But pain, anger, and sorrow so pull him apart that she will have to start his cure with mild applications; stronger medicines come later.*]

VI

When in Phoebus' rays Cancer's
sweltry constellation seethes
who so þan geueþ largely
hys sedes to furrows þat refusen hem
fooled by Ceres' faith
let him gon to acorn trees for corn.
Never in a purple glade
would you look to gader violetz
whan in þe fiers northwyndes
þe felde chirkynge ascrincþ,
ne seke þou nat with gredy hand
the budding vines on lenctne to strip
if grapes you would enjoy;

Autumno potius sua
Bacchus munera contulit.
Signat tempora propriis
Aptans officiis deus
Nec quas ipse coercuit
Misceri patitur vices.
Sic quod praecipiti via
Certum deserit ordinem
Laetos non habet exitus.

in autumpne rather Bacchus
his gifts bestows.
Assigneþ God sesouns
mete to her propre mestiers
nor what courses he hæfþ on wealde
suffers them for to melle.
Thus what on ouerþrowynge wey
forleteþ certayne ordenance,
it has no happy end.

VII

Nubibus atris
Condita nullum
Fundere possunt
Sidera lumen.
Si mare volvens
Turbidus Auster
Misceat aestum,
Vitrea dudum
Parque serenis
Unda diebus
Mox resoluto
Sordida caeno
Visibus obstat.

["Let's start," she says, "with a few questions. Is the world run by chance or by reason?" God rules his works by reason, Boethius answers. "And yet," Philosophy says, "you believe the affairs of men are somehow excluded from divine rule? If God is the beginning of all things, what is their end?" Boethius has forgotten, and forgotten too the nature of humankind and how the universe is governed. This is his sickness: he has lost sight of truth, his vision fogged by delusions.]

VII

With black clouds
hid the heavens
can geten adoun
no light.
If the wod south wind
walwyng þe see
medleþ flodwielm,
glæshluttor ær
like unto clear
days, the water
eft bifoulet
with loosened mud
blocks all sight.

Quique vagatur
Montibus altis
Defluus amnis,
Saepe resistit
Rupe soluti
Obice saxi.
Tu quoque si vis
Lumine claro
Cernere verum,
Tramite recto
Carpere callem,
Gaudia pelle,
Pelle timorem
Spemque fugato
Nec dolor adsit.
Nubila mens est
Vinctaque frenis
Haec ubi regnant.

Hwæt, se broc
ofdæl meandering
fro heye montaygnes
oft is staid
by a dam of stone
slaked off a tor.
You too: if you'd
truth aknowen
wiþ clere lyght,
on þæm rihtryne
a paþ acheesen,
adræf glædnesse
gryre adræf,
fleme þou hope,
ne heer be sorwe—
the mind is clouded
with snaffle bound
where þise regnen ynnne.

Liber II / Book II

I

Haec cum superba verterit vices dextra
Et aestuantis more fertur Euripi,
Dudum tremendos saeva proterit reges
Humilemque victi sublevat fallax vultum
Non illa miseros audit aut curat fletus
Ultroque gemitus dura quos fecit ridet.
Sic illa ludit, sic suas probat vires
Magnumque suis demonstrat ostentum, si quis
Visatur una stratus ac felix hora.

[*After a brief silence, Philosophy observes that Boethius' sick-
ness is caused by his longing for his former good fortune—as if
it ever gave him anything of real worth. With the help of those
gentle medicines, rhetoric and music, Philosophy will remind
him of Fortune's nature: blind, deluding, inconstant. Boethius
should either follow Fortune without complaining or turn away
from what can only lead to grief. "Trust your sails to the winds,
you must go where the winds take you. Give yourself to For-
tune, you have got to submit to her ways. Would you stop
Fortune's wheel? Foolish man: it would be fortune no more."*]

I

When Fortune with haught right hand entrechaungeþ
coursing like the riptide of Euripus,
hwilum cruel, crushes wrawe kings
and raiseth, false, the won man's humble chere,
hereth not wretches ne reccheþ their weeping—
harde eke, what groaning she caused, she derides.
Swa pleyeþ, swa preueþ sche hir myght
to showe her ffolke a wondar great: if anyone's
seen in a single hour both happy and struck prostrate.

II

Si quantas rapidis incitus
    Pontus versat harenas
Aut quot stelliferis edita noctibus
    Caelo sidera fulgent
Tantas fundat opes nec retrahat manum
    Pleno copia cornu,
Humanum miseras haud ideo genus
    Cesset flere querellas.
Quamvis vota libens excipiat deus
    Multi prodigus auri
Et claris avidos ornet honoribus,
    Nil iam parta videntur,

[*Philosphy now speaks in Fortune's name. "Why do men com-*
plain about me? Is what I take back from them indeed their
own? Change is my nature, like the sea and earth and sky—
why should I be constant because of men's greed? I turn my
wheel; I raise them high; I bring them low—it is their com-
mon lot: and the man I desert today may hope for better things
tomorrow":]

II

If swift sands asmoche as the rushing
  sea turneþ upwardes with winds;
or as many constellations ascinaþ
  in the welkyn on starry nights—
thowgh richesse somoche plentee pour
  and from fullist horn withdraweþ nat hir hand,
mankynde for al þat nolde ne cesse
  his wrecched playning to biwaile.
How so a willing god receive their votives
  full prodigal of gold
and gridy folk bedecke with honours clere,
  yet nothing seems to them a gayning,

Sed quaesita vorans saeva rapacitas
    Alios pandit hiatus.
Quae iam praecipitem frena cupidinem
    Certo fine retentent,
Largis cum potius muneribus fluens
    Sitis ardescit habendi?
Numquam dives agit qui trepidus gemens
    Sese credit egentem.

but cruell raveyn, swolwyng þayre þrift,
    stretcheþ oþer chawes.
What brideles wiþholden now hedlong
    desiar to any certeyn ende,
when flowing rather in largesse
    ay brenneþ þe þri&st; of havyng?
He never lives a rich man who fearful, moaning,
    believes himself in need.

III

Cum polo Phoebus roseis quadrigis
     Lucem spargere coeperit,
Pallet albentes hebetata vultus
     Flammis stella prementibus.
Cum nemus flatu zephyri tepentis
     Vernis inrubuit rosis,
Spiret insanum nebulosus auster:
     Iam spinis abeat decus.
Saepe tranquillo radiat sereno
     Immotis mare fluctibus,
Saepe ferventes aquilo procellas
     Verso concitat aequore.

["If Fortune spoke to you like this," asks Philosophy, "what
could you reply?" Fortune's argument is specious, says Boethius;
after her sweet talk is over, grief returns. "Yes, but remember, it
was only meant as a palliative." Philosophy questions Boethius'
self-pity, recalling for him his blessings and honors. Does he
sorrow now that they are gone? Since on the last day of life all
one's fortunes end, what does it signify whether you leave them
or they abandon you?]

III

When Phoebus in welkyn wiþ rosene waynes
    begins to shower light,
dimmed by flames opprissing, se steorra
    paleþ his hwitan wlite.
When the woods with the breath of the warm west wind
    wexen redy with spring roses,
þe wod south wind may blow foggy:
    þan of þorne busk is beautee gone.
Oft þe see on smyltum wedre
    shines unstirred by wawes,
oft the north wind stearce stormas
    whelweþ ouer moeuyng watres.

Rara si constat sua forma mundo,
    Si tantas variat vices,
Crede fortunis hominum caducis,
    Bonis crede fugacibus.
Constat aeterna positumque lege est
    Ut constet genitum nihil.

Yif of the worldes owene forme scarce stands fast,
    yif so many varienges it chaungeþ,
then trust the falling fortunes of men!
    trust in slippar goodz!
Stent on eċe æ and is sett:
    þat no þing born endures.

IV

Quisquis volet perennum
     Cautus ponere sedem
Stabilisque nec sonori
     Sterni flatibus Euri
Et fluctibus minantem
     Curat spernere pontum,
Montis cacuman alti,
     Bibulas vitet harenas.
Illud protervus Auster
     Totis viribus urget,
Hae pendulum solutae
     Pondus ferre recusant.

["True," says Boethius, "I was prosperous once. But of all misfortunes, the unhappiest is to have been happy, once." Philosophy reminds him of the blessings that remain—his father-in-law Symmachus, his wife, and his sons are all safe and well—blessings more precious to him than his own self. And yet, like all men, whatever their condition, he will complain impatiently. Why look outside oneself when eternal happiness lies within, beyond suffering, beyond life or death itself:]

IV

Who wary wyl
        settan eċe setl
and stable, ne caste doune
        by Eurus' roring blastz,
and wil dispise þe see
        manassynge wiþ floodes—
copp þæs hean muntes,
        soking sandes he'll shun:
one þe felle estewynde
        swingþ wiþ alle his strengþes,
toþer lous refuse
        to bear the hanging weight.

Fugiens periculosam
    Sortem sedis amoenae
Humili domum memento
    Certus figere saxo.
Quamvis tonet ruinis
    Miscens aequora ventus,
Tu conditus quieti
    Felix robore valli
Duces serenus aevum
    Ridens aetheris iras.

Fleeing þat perilous
    lot of a myrie seat
remember thy house siker
    to fix on a lowh stoon.
Þough the wind soune
    on hryrum, medelyng the waters,
thou welful, sauf in strengh
    of quietz rampar,
shall lead a life serene,
    deriding þa ierru of þe eir.

V

Felix nimium prior aetas
Contenta fidelibus arvis
Nec inerti perdita luxu,
Facili quae sera solebat
Ieiunia solvere glande.
Non Bacchica munera norant
Liquido confundere melle
Nec lucida vellera Serum
Tyrio miscere veneno.
Somnos dabat herba salubres,
Potum quoque lubricus amnis,
Umbras altissima pinus.
Nondum maris alta secabat

["I think the time has come," says Philosophy, "for somewhat stronger medicine." What in gold, jewels, and money is intrinsically valuable? Their worth is greatest not when they are hoarded but when spent or given away. If you measure your needs by nature, you require very little. The earth, the sea, the sky, the moon and stars are beautiful, but do you insist on possessing them? What humankind claims for its wealth and adornment is trifling, even debasing and harmful—and where is the good in that?]

V

Full blysful was þe raþer age
apayed with trusty plowlands,
not lost in sluggish lust,
wont the fast at euene
to break with ready mæste.
Knew not the Bacchic gifts
to melle wiþ clere hony,
ne scire silken cloths
to dye with Tyro purpur.
Gærs ġeaf ġesundne slæp,
als drynke þe rennyng ryuer,
shade the lofty pine.
No straunger yit acleaf

Nec mercibus undique lectis
Nova litora viderat hospes.
Tunc classica saeva tacebant,
Odiis neque fusus acerbis
Cruor horrida tinxerat arva.
Quid enim furor hosticus ulla
Vellet prior arma movere,
Cum vulnera saeva viderent
Nec praemia sanguinis ulla?
Utinam modo nostra redirent
In mores tempora priscos!
Sed saevior ignibus Aetnae
Fervens amor ardet habendi.
Heu primus quis fuit ille
Auri qui pondera tecti
Gemmasque latere volentes
Pretiosa pericula fodit?

þa heahsæ with choice wares
from aywhere to see new strands.
Whist then were cruel clariouns,
blood yshed by egre hate
had not soaked rough fields.
Hwelċ ærre laþmod wodnes
would any armes rayse,
when savage wounds are seen
and no return for blode?
La! þæt ure tide to oolde
maneres wold retourne!
But fersere than the fires of Etna
brenneþ the fervent love of having.
Eala! what was he þat raþest
æfter hefġum goldhorde,
gems wanting to ben hid,
dalf up pretty perils?

VI

Novimus quantas dederit ruinas
Urbe flammata patribusque caesis
Fratre qui quondam ferus interempto
Matris effuso maduit cruore
Corpus et visu gelidum pererrans
Ora non tinxit lacrimis, sed esse
Censor extincti potuit decoris.
Hic tamen sceptro populos regebat
Quos videt condens radios sub undas
Phoebus extremo veniens ab ortu,
Quos premunt septem gelidi triones,
Quos Notus sicco violentus aestu
Torret ardentes recoquens harenas.

⌈*"As to dignities and power, which you so exalt," Philosophy
continues, "fallen in all ages to the wrong hands, they have
been the cause of more destruction than any volcano or flood."
Clearly such things are not good in themselves but reflect the
character of those who possess them.*⌉

VI

We know how great the ruins he wrought.
Romeburg forbrent, senatours ofslen,
who wild man hys broþer sometyme ymorþred
was bewet wiþ his moder blood yshed
and reviewing her chill cors at the sight
no tere hys chekes ne wessh, but assayed
to critique her dedded beauty.
This man naþelas with scepter peoples ruled
whom Phoebus spies, rays yhid under
yþa rising in the uttrest east,
whom the cold Septemtriones crudaþ,
whom stearc Notus mid searre hæte
scorklith, sithing the burning sandz.

Celsa num tandem valuit potestas
Vertere pravi rabiem Neronis?
Heu gravem sortem, quotiens iniquus
Additur saevo gladius veneno!

Could not at lenghe this lofty power
hwierfan þa wodnesse of prave Nero?
Eala! grevous hap, swa oft unriht
sweord is affixt to cruel venom.

VII

Quicumque solam mente praecipiti petit
        Summumque credit gloriam,
Late patentes aetheris cernat plagas,
        Artumque terrarum situm.
Brevem replere non valentis ambitum
        Pudebit aucti nominis.
Quid o superbi colla mortali iugo
        Frustra levare gestiunt?
Licet remotos fama per populos means
        Diffusa linguas explicet
Et magna titulis fulgeat claris domus,
        Mors spernit altam gloriam,

["You know that mortal ambition held little sway over me,"
says Boethius. "But I did want to engage in public matters, so
that my worth would not silently waste away." Philosophy
responds. The vainglories of the affairs of state have an appeal
for excellent but unperfected minds. Think how small the earth
is in relation to the heavens, how limited the regions inhabited
by man! yet how separate one people is from another, how
"immortal" fame when measured against eternity! Only a
conscious mind free of earthly chains can exult in the happi-
ness of heaven.]

VII

Whoso wiþ ouerþrowynge mode secþ only
        wuldor, believes it alþerbeste,
let him scan the open widland of þe eir
        and of þis erþe þe streite.
His name's increase shall shame him, unable
        to fulfille þe skant compas.
La! the proud, why in idel do they yearn
        to lift from their necks the mortal yoke?
Thogh þat fame y-spradde thorow ferne peoples
        passing onwæfliġe tungan
and a great house wiþ clere honours shine,
        death dispiseþ heah wuldor,

Involvit humile pariter et celsum caput
     Aequatque summis infima.
Ubi nunc fidelis ossa Fabricii manent,
     Quid Brutus aut rigidus Cato?
Signat superstes fama tenuis pauculis
     Inane nomen litteris.
Sed quod decora novimus vocabula,
     Num scire consumptos datur?
Iacetis ergo prorsus ignorabiles
     Nec fama notos efficit.
Quod si putatis longius vitam trahi
     Mortalis aura nominis,
Cum sera vobis rapiet hoc etiam dies,
     Iam vos secunda mors manet.

wæfþ humble heued and lofty alike,
    ġeemnett þe hyhe wiþ þe lowe.
Hwær sint nu þæs triewan Fabricius' ban,
    what is Brutus or ſtiern Caton?
Fragile fame surviving marks with a few
    letters an inane name.
But by cause we onġietaþ faire wordes
    is it yyven us to know the dead?
You lie then to the end unknowe
    ne fame ne makeþ couþ.
For if you think to drawe youre lyf on-long
    with the aura round your mortal name,
when the latter day ġegripþ even this from you,
    then your second death remains.

VIII

Quod mundus stabile fide
Concordes variat vices,
Quod pugnantia semina
Foedus perpetuum tenent,
Quod Phoebus roseum diem
Curru provehit aureo,
Ut quas duxerit Hesperos
Phoebe noctibus imperet,
Ut fluctus avidum mare
Certo fine coerceat,
Ne terris liceat vagis
Latos tendere terminos,
Hanc rerum seriem ligat

["But do not think," says Philosophy, "that I wage impla-
cable war against Fortune." So long as men are not deceived
by the transience of happiness, they may find the wisdom that
lies in adversity and learn from Fortune's false, changing face
what is of real value in life: true friends.]

VIII

That þe world on treowfæstnesse
entrechaungeþ in harmony,
that wiþerwearde ġesċeafta
a healdaþ singale sibbe,
that the sonne the ruddy day
bringþ with his goldene chare,
swa what the even-star hat browt
the moon has gouernance by night,
swa þe wode see his wawes
straitens with a certeyn ende,
þy laes he ġeond woruldsċeatas
mot abræden brade mearcas—
what binds þis ġeræw of things

Terras ac pelagus regens
Et caelo imperitans amor.
Hic si frena remiserit,
Quidquid nunc amat invicem
Bellum continuo geret
Et quam nunc socia fide
Pulchris motibus incitant,
Certent solvere machinam.
Hic sancto populos quoque
Iunctos foedere continet,
Hic et coniugii sacrum
Castis nectit amoribus,
Hic fidis etiam sua
Dictat iura sodalibus.
O felix hominum genus,
Si vestros animos amor
Quo caelum regitur regat.

governynge the land and sea
eke þe heuenes ruling: love.
Love if the bridelis forlæt
what now that she doth interlink
wolden ſtraiſt a werre maken
and now on trewes allyed
in fayre moeuynges aſtir
would fight the fasoun to fordoon.
This love doth hold alswa peoples
ioygned with an hooly sibbe
and the sacrement of wedlok
knytteth of chaſte amouris,
enditeth eke hire owne
lawes to felawes trewe.
La! happy weere humain kind
if the love that rules the heavens
roulide yowre corages.

Liber III / Book III

I

Qui serere ingenuum volet agrum,
Liberat arva prius fruticibus,
Falce rubos filicemque resecat,
Ut nova fruge gravis Ceres eat.
Dulcior est apium mage labor,
Si malus ora prius sapor edat.
Gratius astra nitent ubi Notus
Desinit imbriferos dare sonos.
Lucifer ut tenebras pepulerit
Pulchra dies roseos agit equos.
Tu quoque falsa tuens bona prius
Incipe colla iugo retrahere.
Vera dehinc animum subierint.

["O felix hominum genus,/" Philosophy concludes her song,
"Si vestros animus amor/Quo caelum regitur regat." Boethius
now feels so soothed that he is ready to try her more bitter
medicines. "I thought you were," says Philosophy, "and you
would be even more eager if you understood where I am tak-
ing you." But first she would show him the familiar cause of
deception, so the sight of true happiness might be all the clearer.]

I

Who an æcer unbegan wyl sow
first frees the plowland of þa þornas,
clears fearn and fyrsas wiþ his fauchon,
that Ceres come, heavy with new corn.
Bees' work bese þe more swete
if the mouth first savours bitter smæcc.
Bliþor scinaþ stars where the south wind
cesseþ to blowe his ploungy blasts.
That the morning star adræfþ the dark
fayre day spurs on his ruddy hors.
You too, viewing first false goodes,
gin your neck to draw back fro þe yok,
hennes the true inhielde your heart.

II

Quantas rerum flectat habenas
Natura potens, quibus immensum
Legibus orbem provida servet
Stringatque ligans inresoluto
Singula nexu, placet arguto
Fidibus lentis promere cantu.
Quamvis Poeni pulchra leones
Vincula gestent manibusque datas
Captent escas metuantque trucem
Soliti verbera ferre magistrum,
Si cruor horrida tinxerit ora,
Resides olim redeunt animi
Fremituque gravi meminere sui;

*[Philosophy looks down for a moment to collect her thoughts.
"Happiness," she begins, "is the highest good. Men strive after
it in many ways: through wealth, honor, power, fame, plea-
sure, or these in various combinations—all of which have
some good in themselves and point, therefore, to goodness itself
as the perfect happiness."]*

II

Hu fela the reins of þinges þat myghty
nature guides! yee by whiche lawes
provident the great world ġe wreþaþ
ġe wriþþ, tijnge eallwihta with
vnslacked knot—it luſt to shewe
be schyre songe on supple ſtrings.
Hwæt, þe liouns of Affryke fayre
fetters drawe, tidbits take from feeding
hands, hir grimne mæġeſter adrede
whose whippings they are wont to bere:
if blood besmear hir briſtled mouþes,
corage er ydel repeyreþ agein
and with grevous roar they hemself remember:

Laxant nodis collis solutis
Primusque lacer dente cruento
Domitor rabidas imbuit iras.
Quae canit altis garrula ramis
Ales caveae clauditur antro;
Huic licet inlita pocula melle
Largasque dapes dulci studio
Ludens hominum cura ministret,
Si tamen arto saliens texto
Nemorum gratas viderit umbras,
Sparsas pedibus proterit escas,
Silvas tantum maesta requirit,
Silvas dulci voce susurrat.
Validis quondam viribus acta
Pronum flectit virga cacumen;
Hanc si curvans dextra remisit,
Recto spectat vertice caelum.
Cadit Hesperias Phoebus in undas,
Sed secreto tramite rursus
Currum solitos vertit ad ortus.
Repetunt proprios quaeque recursus
Redituque suo singula gaudent
Nec manet ulli traditus ordo
Nisi quod fini iunxerit ortum
Stabilemque sui fecerit orbem.

from slackened noose hir nekkes hie aliesaþ,
the firſt tamer al to-tore wiþ blody
teeth triggers þere wode wraþþes.
Hwæt, þe jangland bryd that sings on heye
braunches is cooped in a vaulting cage;
though honeyed litel draughts are given hem
and large metes wiþ swete ſtudie
of the pleiyng besines of men,
if hopping on the narwe trelliswork
þilke brid the woods' welcome shade espies,
tredaþ he skatterd taſties underfote,
sorgfull langaþ æfter the foreſt alone,
hwispreþ with his swete voys: "foreſt."
The sapling eek, once by mighty fors
askew niþerweard wrenċeþ his copp;
if þat þe hond þat hente remit,
upriht þe cropp ſtaraþ to sky weard.
Þuswise Phoebus in weſtren wawes falz
but by a priue paþe underbæc
to his wonted arysing hwierſþ his wæġn.
Eallwihta seken ayein hir propre cours
and of hir owne retours reiosen hem
ne noon ordenaunce to nanwihte is
given but joyneth ende to begynnyng
and makeþ of himself a cercle trewe.

III

Quamvis fluente dives auri gurgite
    Non expleturas cogat avarus opes
Oneretque bacis colla rubri litoris
    Ruraque centeno scindat opima bove,
Nec cura mordax deseret superstitem,
    Defunctumque leves non comitantur opes.

["As in a dream," says Philosophy, "you men have a vague
sense of the happiness in your beginning and your end. You
seek it in, say, riches, which smack of goodness by alleviating
some of life's difficulties. But when you were wealthy, were
you also free from care?" "Of course not." "You either desired
something more or feared that something might be taken from
you." "Yes." "And therefore you needed help in holding on to
what you had: so much for the self-sufficiency of riches!"]

III

A rich covetour: how somoche in a riuer rennyng
        with gold he gadriġe unfulfulling fee,
yee his nekke charge wiþ pearls of Reddis Sea
        and harrow æcera cyst each wiþ an hundreþ ox,
naþelas gnawyng cure him cwicne ne forlæt,
        deadne his dysiġa feoh ne mid him a gæþ.

IV

Quamvis se Tyrio superbus ostro
  Comeret et niveis lapillis,
Invisus tamen omnibus vigebat
  Luxuriae Nero saevientis.
Sed quondam dabat improbus verendis
  Patribus indecores curules.
Quis illos igitur putet beatos
  Quos miseri tribuunt honores?

["Concerning the honor accrued through the dignity of office,"
Philosophy goes on, "*it is in the end of no account. The respect
of office is not automatic—in point of fact, it is lowered by
corruption; neither does it endure the ages nor have much sig-
nificance abroad, among foreigners.*"]

IV

Thogh he makeþ it proude wiþ purpure
    Tyriene and pearls of snowy white,
loothly to alle folk, naþelas he throf,
    Nero, in his woode luxurie.
Hwæt, he wamfull hwilum ġeaf to arworthy
    senatours unworthy curule chayers.
Who would then suppose swiche honours blisfull
    for to bene, by shrewes bestowne?

V

Qui se volet esse potentem
Animos domet ille feroces
Nec victa libidine colla
Foedis submittat habenis.
Etenim licet Indica longe
Tellus tua iura tremescat
Et serviat ultima Thyle,
Tamen atras pellere curas
Miserasque fugare querelas
Non posse potentia non est.

["And what of the power of kings?" asks Philosophy. "What kind of power is it that fears most for its preservation? Remember the sword of Damocles! And if a king's position seems tenuous, think of his retainers and those among them he counts as friends—more plague than friendship when in misfortune these friends become enemies."]

V

Who þæt wolde myghty for to been
mot his wilde mod atemian
nor loſt to lecherye ne his neck
underlicgan to swich foul reines.
Yea although þæt feorr Indisċe
land quakith at þi lawes
and ultima Thule be þral to þe,
hwæþre derk desijres adræfan
eke afliegan wrecched playning
næfþ þu no power to doon.

VI

Omne hominum genus in terris simili surgit ab ortu.
Unus enim rerum pater est, unus cuncta ministrat.
Ille dedit Phoebo radios dedit et cornua lunae,
Ille homines etiam terris dedit ut sidera caelo,
Hic clausit membris animos celsa sede petitos.
Mortales igitur cunctos edit nobile germen.
Quid genus et proavos strepitis? Si primordia vestra
Auctoremque deum spectes, nullus degener exstat,
Ni vitiis peiora fovens proprium deserat ortum.

*[She continues. "Glory and fame are false and degrading.
What value is there in a popular reputation? If mistaken, it is
embarrassing; if true, what can it give to a man of conscience,
who himself is the measure of his own worth? Either way, like
honor, it will hardly signify abroad. Nobility? merely a reflec-
tion of your parents' fame. If it has any value, it comes from
trying to live up to your ancestors' reputed virtue."]*

VI

Al humain kind in erþe ben of semblable burþe.
One eke is father of þinges, an ġewielt ealles.
He yaf to þe sonne hys bemes, yaf to þe moone hir hornes,
to the earth gave he men, as stars to the welken,
hir sawla broht of heahsetle he bewriþþ on lime.
Æpele sæd forsoþ alle mortal folk forþbirþ.
Why crake of stock and forme-fadres? If youre begynnynges
þou looke and god þe makere, nan mann nis unæþele,
unles with vice he fede orwierþe and forlete his propre burþe.

VII

Habet hoc voluptas omnis,
Stimulis agit fruentes
Apiumque par volantum
Ubi grata mella fudit,
Fugit et nimis tenaci
Ferit icta corda morsu.

["And as for bodily pleasures, think of the anxiety and regret they cause, their fruit of disease and pain. Are men as beasts, whose only happiness is physical satisfaction? Even a wife and family can be a torment; as Euripides once said, who wants for children, call him fortunate in his misfortune."]

VII

Alle luſt haþ þis:
chaceþ injoyars wiþ prikkes,
and like the flying bee
hys gladsom honies shad
oþfliehþ and þe herte aflight
ſtingþ mid ſtiċe too langsum faſt.

VIII

Eheu quae miseros tramite devios
        Abducit ingorantia!
Non aurum in viridi quaeritis arbore
        Nec vite gemmas carpitis,
Non altis laqueos montibus abditis
        Ut pisce ditetis dapes
Nec vobis capreas si libeat sequi,
        Tyrrhena captatis vada.
Ipsos quin etiam fluctibus abditos
        Norunt recessus aequoris,
Quae gemmis niveis unda feracior
        Vel quae rubentis purpurae
Nec non quae tenero pisce vel asperis

["*Wealth, honor, power, fame, pleasure—all these,*" *Philoso-*
phy concludes, "are stray paths to happiness, confounded with
evils. None leads where it promises, none in itself embodies all
goodness."]

VIII

Eala! what unwit miswent wandryng
  wrecches from their way.
You seek not gold in a green tree
  nor gems pluck off the vine,
ne hydaþ nan nett on heahmuntum
  your dische with fische to fil,
ne yif yow lykeþ to hunte to roos
  would serche Tyrrhen shallows.
Huru, felen in þe floodes folk
  þa hydels of the sea—
wæter forþbærran of snowy pearls
  or rede purpre deye
ġe strand la hwær hnesċe fisċas

Praestent echinis litora.
Sed quonam lateat quod cupiunt bonum,
      Nescire caeci sustinent,
Et quod stelliferum trans abiit polum,
      Tellure demersi petunt.
Quid dignum stolidis mentibus inprecer?
      Opes honores ambiant;
Et cum falsa gravi mole paraverint,
      Tum vera cognoscant bona.

    habounden or harsk seaſtars.
But where lies hid þæs godes hie wilniaþ
    blind þei byden unwar,
and what þurhfareþ þe ſterry heuenes
    they seek in buried ground.
Which heſt shall I for dull mindz make?
    For wealth and honors ſtrive:
whan heavy carke the falz hath got,
    þan con þe verray good.

IX

O qui perpetua mundum ratione gubernas
Terrarum caelique sator qui tempus ab aevo
Ire iubes stabilisque manens das cuncta moveri,
Quem non externae pepulerunt fingere causae
Materiae fluitantis opus, verum insita summi
Forma boni livore carens, tu cuncta superno
Ducis ab exemplo, pulchrum pulcherrimus ipse
Mundum mente gerens similique in imagine formans
Perfectasque iubens perfectum absolvere partes.
Tu numeris elementa ligas ut frigora flammis
Arida conveniant liquidis, ne purior ignis
Evolet aut mersas deducant pondera terras.
Tu triplicis mediam naturae cuncta moventem

["The nature of true happiness is indivisible," says Philoso-
phy, "but as we see, men perceive it only in parts." Striving
after these parts—mere images of a seamless, self-sufficient
whole—they of course gain nothing. Boethius now under-
stands, with Plato, that only with divine help can the seat of
the highest good be revealed. "Just so," agrees Philosophy, and
at once begins to sing:]

IX

La þu! þe weltst þære worulde by resoun lasting;
eorþan ġe heofona sċieppend þe tid fram fruman
hæst for to gon: stedfast and stable all elz astyrest,
whom foreyn causes forst not to frame
werk of floterynge mater, but lo form innate
of soueryn good sanz despit—thou all by high
ensample lætst, self alþerfairest þe faire
worlde beryng on mode and of like mold forming,
bidding this perfeċtion fulle hys perfeċt parties.
Þu bintst þa ġesċeafta by noumbre þætte dryġe ċeald
with liquid flames convene, þy læs the purer fire
offleoge or whelmèd lands be pressed by waights.
Þu ġegadrast the soul þat meveþ all, nature's

Coneﬅens animam per consona membra resolvis.
Quae cum seﬅa duos motum glomeravit in orbes,
In semet reditura meat mentemque profundam
Circuit et simili convertit imagine caelum.
Tu causis animas paribus vitasque minores
Provehis et levibus sublimes curribus aptans
In caelum terrarumque seris quas lege benigna
Ad te conversas reduci facis igne reverti.
Da pater auguﬅam menti conscendere sedem,
Da fontem luﬅrare boni, da luce reperta
In te conspicuos animi defigere visus.
Dissice terrenae nebulas et pondera molis
Atque tuo splendore mica! Tu namque serenum,
Tu requies tranquilla piis, te cernere finis,
Principium, veﬅor, dux, semita, terminus idem.

threefold mean, ġe hie tolieſt on dælum ġeþwærum.
Þus diuided the motion nearwaþ into speres two,
on hire selfre retourneth and þæt deop mod
bisetz, whielyng in like mold þe welken.
Þu by euenlyk causes souls and lesser lives
forþbirſt, and ablyng þa hiehſt in swifteſt wains
sæweſt hem in heuen and erþe—þurh fremsume æ
þa ilcan to þe aċierred, tyrneſt eft with fire redux.
Let the mynd, la fæder! mounte þin heahsetl,
let hym luſtre at þe welle of good, in that light
yfounde let him ficchen in þe the soul's clear sight.
Todrif the miſts and waights of erthely pays,
schyne þou eek by þi bryhtnes! Þu hlutor lyft,
thou softe reſt to þæm rihtwisum, thee to behold their aim:
Fruma. Berere. Wisa. Anpæþ. Eċe ende.

X

Huc omnes pariter venite capti
Quos fallax ligat improbis catenis
Terrenas habitans libido mentes,
Haec erit vobis requies laborum,
Hic portus placida manens quiete,
Hoc patens unum miseris asylum.
Non quidquid Tagus aureis harenis
Donat aut Hermus rutilante ripa
Aut Indus calido propinquus orbi
Candidis miscens virides lapillos,
Inlustrent aciem magisque caecos
In suas condunt animos tenebras.
Hoc quidquid placet excitatque mentes,

["You seek the seat of the highest good," repeats Philosophy, "and hope to find it in imperfect reflections." Imperfection implies the existence of perfection, the totality of all things: God. Here is the seat and the very substance of the highest good: the greatest happiness.]

X

Come all ye ycaught hider ætgædere
whom that fals lust inhabytaunt of erthely
myndz mid wamfullum feterum ġebindeþ,
þis shal ben þe reste of youre laboures,
here a haven lasting calme and stille,
this alone þe refut ouert to wrecches.
Ne swa hwæt from golden sandz þe ryuere
Tagus yields or Hermus from his rede brenk
or Indus next þæm wearman woruldsċeate
medlyng gemstones, smaragdes wiþ margarits—
ne onlihtaþ hi naught sċearpnesse, hydaþ
hie rather in their penumbra blindid souls.
What you here find pleasaunt, what excites the mind,

Infimis tellus aluit cavernis;
Splendor quo regitur vigetque caelum,
Vitat obscuras animae ruinas.
Hanc quisquis poterit notare lucem,
Candidos Phoebi radios negabit.

erþe haþ noryshed in hys lowest caves;
that light werbi þe welken is ruled and thrives
onsċunaþ hit þæs modes mierce hryras.
Ġif hwelċ mon ġesion mæġe þa birhtu,
hwæt! the sun's clear radiance he will deny.

XI

Quisquis profunda mente vestigat verum
Cupitque nullis ille deviis falli,
In se revolvat intimi lucem visus
Longosque in orbem cogat inflectens motus
Animumque doceat quidquid extra molitur
Suis retrusum possidere thesauris.
Dudum quod atra texit erroris nubes
Lucebit ipso perspicacius Phoebo.
Non omne namque mente depulit lumen
Obliviosam corpus invehens molem.
Haeret profecto semen introrsum veri
Quod excitatur ventilante doctrina.
Nam cur rogati sponte recta censetis,

["*What we call good,*" *Philosophy continues, "is good inso-
far as it partakes of goodness and becomes one with its sub-
stance." Whatever lives survives by maintaining its unity; when
the vital parts separate, it dies. Whatever exists aspires after
its integrity, that is to say, the highest good. Boethius agrees.
"Then," says Philosophy, "you remember at last what you
said you had forgotten." "What is that?" "The end of all
things."*]

XI

Who so that sekith soth by a deep thoght
and nylle by no mis-weyes to ben misled,
turne he hym self to the light of ynnere eyen,
large discours wrying reſtreyne in compas,
yee lere his corage what so he secþ
to hold in keep ġemang his agene maþmas.
Æeror hwæt sweart ġedwolmiſt hydde
shall shine forth sċiror þan þe sonne hym self.
The body hauling its forgetful hulk
al mindz light ne hath not todrifen.
Certes som seed of sooth clyueth with-ynne
þæt wierþ aweht in the breeze of learning's air.
Forwhy when axed demen ye wilfullye the ryhtes

Ni mersus alto viveret fomes corde?
Quod si Platonis musa personat verum,
Quod quisque discit immemor recordatur.

save the tinder live besenċed on breoſthorde.
Because if Plato's muse syngeth sooth,
hwæt mon onġiett forġietol he ġeman.

XII

Felix qui potuit boni
Fontem visere lucidum,
Felix qui potuit gravis
Terrae solvere vincula.
Quondam funera coniugis
Vates Threicius gemens
Postquam flebilibus modis
Silvas currere mobiles,
Amnes stare coegerat,
Iunxitque intrepidum latus
Saevis cerva leonibus,
Nec visum timuit lepus,
Iam cantu placidum canem,

["I very much agree with Plato," says Boethius, "truth is knowledge that our souls have forgotten." "Now if you consider further," Philosophy tells him, "you will recall what else you could not remember: how the universe is governed." Boethius affirms that a single entity, which he calls "God," brings the discordant parts of the world into working harmony. Philosophy resumes: God, as we have seen, is the highest good and greatest happiness, and so rules all things with kindly power; while evil is insubstantial, since it lies outside the divine sphere. This is not empty argument; as Plato once again says, words are akin to what they speak of.]

XII

Blisful he who mæġ ġeseon
þone hluttran æwelm of good,
blisful he who mæġ þa bendas
onlætan of heuy erþe.
In ġear-dagum the Thracian bard
þe deeþ of hys wijf waymenting,
afterward with weeply songes
made the quickened woods to renne,
þe stremes to stonden stille,
and joyned dredles side by side
þe hynde wiþ liouns felle,
yee þe hare was not agast
to see þe hound, now soothèd by song.

Cum flagrantior intima
Fervor pectoris ureret,
Nec qui cuncta subegerant
Mulcerent dominum modi,
Inmites superos querens
Infernas adiit domos.
Illic blanda sonantibus
Chordis carmina temperans
Quidquid praecipuis deae
Matris fontibus hauserat,
Quod luctus dabat impotens,
Quod luctum geminans amor,
Deflet Taenara commovens
Et dulci veniam prece
Umbrarum dominos rogat.
Stupet tergeminus novo
Captus carmine ianitor,
Quae sontes agitant metu
Ultrices scelerum deae
Iam maestae lacrimus madent.
Non Ixionium caput
Velox praecipitat rota
Et longa site perditus
Spernit flumina Tantalus.
Vultur dum satur est modis,
Non traxit Tityi iecur.
Tandem, "Vincimur," arbiter
Umbrarum miserans ait,

While ferventar yearning byrnyd
þus innanweard Orpheus' breast
soncræft þe eallwihta weold
would not pacefie þe maister:
hearde heofonware plaining
wente to the hous of helle.
Þere hys blaundissyng songes
wiþ resounyng strenges blende
(alle þat he'd laued out hys
goddes modres noble welles
sorwynge sanz restrain brought forth,
loue þat doubelyth sorwe)
he weeps, hellegeat commoevyng
and with dulce suite a pardon
asks the lords of sceaduhelme.
Stunned se þri-heafdede geatweard
wæs, captive of unwonted song,
now the goddess vengerisses
who vexe felowns wiþ feere
sor were wiþ teres wepyng.
Ixion his head is whirled not
by þe ouerþrowing whele,
and Tantalus by þrust forlost
wolde ofshowve the waters.
While the gryph glutted mid gliwe
tereþ nat Tityus' mawe.
"We are overcome," æftercwiþþ
þe juge of shadwes pitying,

"Donamus comitem viro
Emptam carmine coniugem.
Sed lex dona coerceat,
Ne, dum Tartara liquerit,
Fas sit lumina flectere."
Quis legem det amantibus?
Maior lex amor est sibi.
Heu, noctis prope terminos
Orpheus Eurydicen suam
Vidit, perdidit, occidit.
Vos haec fabula respicit
Quicumque in superum diem
Mentem ducere quaeritis.
Nam qui Tartareum in specus
Victus lumina flexerit,
Quidquid praecipuum trahit
Perdit, dum videt inferos.

"yyve we þis man his fere,
his wijf þus wonnen wiþ his song.
But let þis yift a law restrain:
ne may he, as from hell he goes,
cast an eye underbæc næfre."
Who can make a law for lovers?
Love to itself is stronger law.
Weilawei! near the end of night
Orpheus his Eurydice
onseah, forleas, acwealde þus.
Þis bispell perteyneth to yow
þat in to souereyne day
secþ modġepoht to lædenne.
Who on hellscræfe overcome
would cast hys eyen underbæc,
al þat he haþ drawen of worþ
forlyst he, þa he niþer siehþ.

Liber IV / Book IV

I

Sunt etenim pennae volucres mihi
        Quae celsa conscendant poli,
Quas sibi cum velox mens induit,
        Terras perosa despicit,
Aeris inmensi superat globum,
        Nubesque postergum videt,
Quique agili motu calet aetheris,
        Transcendit ignis verticem,
Donec in astriferas surgat domos
        Phoeboque coniungat vias
Aut comitetur iter gelidi senis
        Miles corusci sideris,
Vel quocumque micans nox pingitur,

[Boethius, continuing to be gnawed by grief, breaks in as Phi-
losophy concludes her song. "Yes, the ruler of all things is good.
What astonishes me then is: not only can evil still exist, it
flourishes unchecked!" It would be awful, Philosophy responds,
if that were really so. But in fact that is not so, as she will
show him. She will give Boethius' mind wings to fly back to
his true homeland.]

I

Hwæt, ic self hæbbe feþera swifte
      that scale þe heyhte of heuene,
cloþed in which þanne þæt hræþe mod
      looks down on the earth with loathing,
rises above þe spere of infynyt eir
      and siehþ þa wolcnu under,
yee hoot in the aether's rapid mouyng
      surmounteþ þæs fyres mearce,
til þe sterry houses it ascende
      and join with Phoebus' paths,
or fare old cold Saturn's road,
      þe clere planetes knyht,
efne aywhere the shining night is deckt

Recurrat astri circulum;
Atque ubi iam exhausti fuerit satis,
    Polum relinquat extimum
Dorsaque velocis premat aetheris
    Compos verendi luminis.
Hic regum sceptrum dominus tenet
    Orbisque habenas temperat
Et volucrem currum stabilis regit
    Rerum coruscus arbiter.
Huc te si reducem referat via,
    Quam nunc requiris immemor:
"Haec," dices, "memini, patria est mihi.
    Hinc ortus, hic sistam gradum."
Quod si terrarum placeat tibi
    Noctem relictam visere,
Quos miseri torvos populi timent
    Cernes tyrannos exules.

renne þa rynne of stars—
now when it hath ynough fullfylling
    forleteþ heuene ferrest,
and hard upon the back of coursing aether
    behielt þæt wundorleoht.
Heer þe lorde of kynges his ceptre halt
    and raines of the worlde doth gide,
þæm hrædwæġne stioreþ he, stedfast,
    clere juge of þinges.
Hider if the way bring thee redux,
    which sekestow forġietol,
"Þes," you'll say remembering, "is eþel and origin,
    her iċ stæppe fæste."
An it please thee then earth's forlætenne
    niht to oferseonne,
grym tyrauntes þat wrecchede folk ondrædaþ
    beon ġesihst þu wreċċan.

II

Quos vides sedere celsos solii culmine reges
Purpura claros nitente saeptos tristibus armis
Ore torvo comminantes rabie cordis anhelos,
Detrahat si quis superbis vani tegmina cultus,
Iam videbit intus artas dominos ferre catenas.
Hinc enim libido versat avidis corda venenis,
Hinc flagellat ira mentem fluctus turbida tollens
Maeror aut captus fatigat aut spes lubrica torquet.
Ergo cum caput tot unum cernas ferre tyannos,
Non facit quod optat ipse dominis pressus iniquis.

["Through volition and power," says Philosophy, "people ob-
tain what they want." In striving for the highest good, the
weakness of evil becomes clear: it cannot achieve the greatest
happiness, egged on by trifling desires. An evil man in his
blind ignorance is like a corpse, a semblance of humanity, a
nullity powerless and without will. Philosophy cites Plato
again: wise men can do what they wish; the wicked carry out
their actions perforce, never to fulfill their yearnings.]

II

Heahcyningas þu sihst sittan on þæm heahsetlum
florishing with purple fayre, with dour armes enuyrond,
thretyng with dredfull looke, for hartz yre acheked—
who so þat strepe the proud of her trappings of veyn array
ġesiehþ þa hlafordas beraþ la! streyte bondis wiþ-ynne.
Hennes lust certein hiera heortan wrenċeþ with ravynous venyms,
hennes wrath þæt mod swingþ, wild storm raising,
or sorwe werieth hem ycaught or slippar hopes worry.
Þus syn þou seest oo heed so many a tyrant bears,
he doth not what he wold, be harde maisters prest.

III

Vela Neritii ducis
Et vagas pelago rates
Eurus appulit insulae,
Pulchra qua residens dea
Solis edita semine
Miscet hospitibus novis
Tacta carmine pocula.
Quos ut in varios modos
Vertit herbipotens manus,
Hunc apri facies tegit,
Ille Marmaricus leo
Dente crescit et unguibis.
Hic lupis nuper additius,

["You see now," says Philosophy, "the muck in which vil-
lainy wallows and the radiant light of goodness. Each is its
own reward." The reward of happiness that comes with good-
ness makes gods of men, a truth no evil can destroy; while the
price of wickedness is to turn men into beasts.]

III

Þe sayles of Aulixes duc
and hys shippes astray at sea
the east wind blewh to þat ile
where Circe dwelling, goddess fair,
of sunnan sæde acenned,
medlyþ to hir newe gestes
pociouns mid balocræftum made.
Hwæt, hire wyrtcræftigan hand
him forsciepþ as in divers ways,
this one bares hiw ymbwindeþ,
that one a lyoun Marmoryk
wiþ tosk and clawe ywoxen.
Þes ġemang wulfum nu ytald,

Flere dum parat, ululat.
Ille tigris ut Indica
Tecta mitis obambulat.
Sed licet variis malis
Numen Arcadis alitis
Obsitum miserans ducem
Peste solverit hospitis,
Iam tamen mala remiges
Ore pocula traxerant,
Iam sues Cerealia
Glande pabula verterant
Et nihil manet integrum
Voce corpore perditis.
Sola mens stabilis super
Monstra quae patitur gemit.
O levem nimium manum
Nec potentia gramina,
Membra quae valeant licet,
Corda vertere non valent!
Intus est hominum vigor
Arce conditus abdita.
Haec venena potentius
Detrahunt hominem sibi
Dira quae penitus meant
Nec nocentia corpori
Mentis vulnere saeviunt.

whan wepe he wolde, he howls.
Þat as an Indian tiger
debonair ín þe hous romeþ.
Al thogh mid mislicum yflum
byseged, godhed Mercurie
pitying þe duc Aulixes
from the geſtz plague him alieseþ,
naþelas nu on wicked cup
þe maryners by mouth had supt,
swyne alswa Ceres mete
hadden for mæſte ichaunged,
yee non ne dwelliþ vnwemmed,
hire voys wiþ cors forloren.
Mynd alone ſtaþolfæſt bufan
whan the monſtars it suffars, wailes.
La! Circes ouer feble hond,
ne here myghty herbes eek,
be it so þei lymes welden,
noght-for-that may not alter hartz.
Innanweard monna ſtrengþu liþ
in secre ſtronge hold yhid.
Thos venoms there are with more fors
þat to hem-ward men todrawe,
dredfull hie þurhfaraþ deope,
and to þe body noyous nat
yit wooden by wounde of myndz.

IV

Quid tantos iuvat excitare motus
    Et propria fatum sollicitare manu?
Si mortem petitis, propinquat ipsa
    Sponte sua volucres nec remorator equos.
Quos serpens leo tigris ursus aper
    Dente petunt, idem se tamen ense petunt.
An distant quia dissidentque mores,
    Iniustas acies et fera bella movent
Alternisque volunt perire telis?
    Non est iusta satis saevitiae ratio.
Vis aptam meritis vicem referre?
    Dilige iure bonos et miseresce malis.

["Granted," says Boethius, "that evil men are but beasts in human guise, they still have it in their means to do terrible harm." "Not really so," Philosophy responds, "as I will show you in due course. The wicked in any case—who feel frustrated by their very achievements—would themselves suffer less if that power you suppose is theirs is removed." The burden of evil being its own reward, it must fall heaviest on evildoers, not on their victims. Just punishment helps relieve them of their burden, sick and pitiful as they are.]

IV

What helpeþ it to hrerenne swelċe unstilnesse
    and wiþ youre propre hond to worry wyrd?
Secst þu deaþ? It drawe hym ny
    selfwilles, ne tarieþ nat hys swifte hors.
Whom serpent, lion, tigre, beere, and boore
    wiþ tosk do seake, lo the same with sword pursue.
For þat mores ben divers and distant,
    are men moved to unrihte werre and vil bataile,
willing by enterchaungyng dartes to die?
    Þe resoun of cruelte nis nat riht ġenoh.
Fit mede wilt þou give desartz?
    Efne lufa þa godu, mildsa þæm yfelum.

V

Si quis Arcturi nescit
    Propinqua summo cardine labi,
Cur legat tardus plaustra Bootes
    Mergatque seras aequore flammas,
Cum nimis celeres explicet ortus,
    Legem stupebit aetheris alti.
Palleant plenae cornua lunae
    Infecta metis noctis opacae
Quaeque fulgenti texerat ore
    Confusa Phoebe detegat astra,
Commovet gentes publicus error
    Lassantque crebris pulsibus aera.
Nemo miratur flamina Cori

["Even so," says Boethius, "bad fortune falling to the wise—
and the reverse, good fortune to the wicked—is hard to bear,
when you consider the power a ruler has, particularly over
prisoners." That this is the work of a just God astonishes him
more than if laws and punishments were meted out fortuitously,
simply by chance. "You think so, and no wonder," Philosophy
responds. "Things will seem accidental and chaotic unless one
knows how they are ordered."]

V

He þat knoweth not Arcturus' star
        dooth neye to þe senyth glyde,
ne hwy slæc Boetes trails the wains
        and sinks late lemes in þe see—
when all too soon arisynge moot vnfolde,
        he wundraþ þære æ of heye eyre.
Waniaþ þe hornes of þe fulle mone
        mid nihtglomes mearcum ġeblanden
and what she had by clere visage ycouered
        Phoebe eclipsed as stars decouereþ:
common error moeueþ folk to rescue,
        werġap with rapid beating brass.
No man no wondreþ whan the northwest wind

Litus frementi tundere fluctu
Nec nivis duram frigore molem
    Fervente Phoebi solvier aestu.
Hic enim causas cernere promptum est,
    Illic latentes pectora turbant.
Cuncta quae rara provehit aetas
    Stupetque subitis mobile vulgus,
Cedat inscitiae nubilus error,
    Cessent profecto mira videri.

      pounds the shore wiþ sounyng flod
nor that snowy clot heard froren
      feruent heat of sun resolues.
Her soþ þa þing swutolu beoþ,
      þær ġehydd breoſt onſtyriaþ.
In our age all þat falleþ seld
      and sodenly þe unsad people ſtuns;
but yif unwisnesse cloud of folly pass,
      the same shall cease merveillous to be.

VI

Si vis celsi iura tonantis
Pura sollers cernere mente,
Aspice summi culmina caeli.
Illic iusto foedere rerum
Veterem servant sidera pacem.
Non sol rutilo concitus igne
Gelidum Phoebes impedit axem
Nec quae summo vertice mundi
Flectit rapidos Ursa meatus,
Numquam occiduo lota profundo
Cetera cernens sidera mergi
Cupit oceano tingere flammas.
Semper vicibus temporis aequis

["Exactly," says Boethius. "And what lies hidden and unex-
plained is what troubles me most." Philosophy smiles. "You
are asking me to look with you into the weightiest matters, in
a brief span of time. Very well then." Divine mind creates and
orders all things. Call this framework "providence"—whose
everyday dispositon is "fate." As understanding is to reason,
the center to a circle, eternity to time, so is providence to fate.
All is purposeful in the changeless plan. In the larger perspec-
tive of good, there would appear to be no evils.]

VI

Yif þou wis mid hlutre mode wilt
þæs heahþunres æ onġietan,
beheald þa hrofas þæs hean heofnes.
There by ryhtful friþe of keende
the constellations keep hir olde pees.
The sun hasted by his ruddy fyre
ne letteþ nat Phoebe's chill axill,
nor at worldes souereyne heyht
doth the Bear her hræde rynas bend,
never wasshen in the westren deep,
seeing there other stars yplounged,
nyll hir lemes sowse not in to occian.
Ever with even turnings of time

Vesper seras nuntiat umbras
Revehitque diem Lucifer almum.
Sic aeternos reficit cursus
Alternus amor, sic astrigeris
Bellum discors exulat oris.
Haec concordia temperat aequis
Elementa modis, ut pugnantia
Vicibus cedant umida siccis
Iungantque fidem frigora flammis,
Pendulus ignis surgat in altum
Terraeque graves pondere sidant.
Isdem causis vere tepenti
Spirat florifer annus odores,
Aestas Cererem fervida siccat,
Remeat pomis gravis autumnus,
Hiemem defluus inrigat imber.
Haec temperies alit ac profert
Quidquid vitam spirat in orbe.
Eadem rapiens condit et aufert
Obitu mergens orta supremo.
Sedet interea conditor altus
Rerumque regens flectit habenas
Rex et dominus fons et origo
Lex et sapiens arbiter aequi
Et quae motu concitat ire,
Sistit retrahens ac vaga firmat.
Nam nisi rectos revocans itus
Flexos iterum cogat in orbes,

bodaþ Hesper þa æfensċuwan
and Lucifer eft ġebringþ bliþne dæġ.
Þus entrelaced loue renews
eternal courses, þus discordaunt
war is outlawid in the ſtarry vale.
This armonie by meet mesure
the elementz attempreþ: flitfull
wæta to dryġe by turns gives way
and ċeald mid hæto joyneþ in feiþ,
hanging fire ariſt on uprodor
ġe hefiġe eorþe þær niþre sitt.
By seluesame cause on wearmum lenċtne
bloſtma tid his sauors doth give bræþ,
sumorhæte dryġeþ Ceres' wheat,
comth ayein hærfeſt heuy of fruyt,
downpouring reġen wætraþ winter-tid.
Þis attemperaunce fett and forþbringþ
al þing in this world that life enspireþ.
Þilke same rauyssing miþþ and nimþ
away, drencheþ upspring on endsete.
Þa hwile sit se hehſta sċeppend,
ruling he welt the raynes of the world.
Cyning and hlaford. Font and fruma.
Lawe and wise juge of equite.
Yee swilke by ſtyrring as he rayses
then backdrawing ſtayes, wandrings eke makes faſt.
For unless rihtrynas recleyming
he ne gadreþ eft in roundes bent,

Quae nunc stabilis continet ordo
Dissaepta suo fonte fatiscant.
Hic est cunctis communis amor
Repetuntque boni fine teneri,
Quia non aliter durare queant,
Nisi converso rursus amore
Refluant causae quae dedit esse.

holden now by stable ordenaunce,
hiera wellsprynges sċeard wold tocleve.
This is the love all ġesċeafta share,
fyn of good they turn to be held by,
ellys ne myhten þei nat endure:
la! þurh wendre lufe onġean-
flowende to the cause that made them be.

VII

Bella bis quinis operatus annis
Ultor Atrides Phrygiae ruinis
Fratris amisssos thalamos piavit;
Ille dum Graiae dare vela classi
Optat et ventos redimit cruore,
Exuit patrem miserumque tristis
Foederat natae iugulum sacerdos.
Flevit amissos Ithacus sodales
Quos ferus vasto recubans in antro
Mersit inmani Polyphemus alvo;
Sed tamen caeco furibundus ore
Gaudium maestis lacrimis rependit.
Herculem duri celebrant labores.

["*You see from this,*" *Philosophy concludes, "that all fortune is in every way good." "How so?" Fortune, no matter happy or sad, is both reward and trial for the virtuous and, for the wicked, corrective punishment. How you meet your fortune, as adversity or opportunity, is your own choice. Its shape is in your hands.*]

VII

Hwæt, Atrides wrecend, Phrygia ruined
æfter werre of yerys twyes fyue,
his broþor forlætenne brydbur revenged;
he while hoissing sails of þe Grekysshe scipps
bæd and bohte þa windas be bloddrynce,
put aside fæder and heard preost the bargain
bledsode wiþ his doghter drery þrote.
Aulixes wepyd his felawes ylorn,
whom lying in þe grete den hadde fiers
Pholifemus freten in his savage panche;
naþeles wood for his blinde visage
he yeld Itakus ioye with wofull teers.
Harde trauyles heryhe Hercules.

Ille Centauros domuit superbos,
Abstulit saevo spolium leoni
Fixit et certis volucres sagittis,
Poma cernenti rapuit draconi
Aureo laevam gravior metallo,
Cerberum traxit triplici catena.
Victor immitem posuisse fertur
Pabulum saevis dominum quadrigis.
Hydra combusto periit veneno,
Fronte turpatus Achelous amnis
Ora demersit pudibunda ripis.
Stravit Antaeum Libycis harenis,
Cacus Evandri satiavit iras
Quosque pressurus foret altus orbis
Saetiger spumis umeros notavit.
Ultimus caelum labor inreflexo
Sustulit collo pretiumque rursus
Ultimi caelum meruit laboris.
Ite nunc fortes ubi celsa magni
Ducit explempli via! Cur inertes
Terga nudatis? Superata tellus
                Sidera donat.

He oferwann þe Centauris swa hauteyn,
the hide of cruell Nemean lyoun flead,
with certain shafts Stymphalian birdz did hit,
golden apples from the watchful dragoun reft
hys hand þe more heuy for þe the metal,
dog Cerberus drough he by trebill cheyne.
Victor, he fedde fell Dyomed, is said,
for fodre to hir maistres wilde wain hors.
Hydra forwearþ, hire venym all forbrent.
Forheed defowled, Achelous þe flod
his shame-face forhydde on his ea strande.
Antaeus he strake under Libyan sands,
wiþ Cacus deeþ Evander's wrothe he pesid,
and þa sculdru þe heye spere sholde
þrest the bristled boar wiþ scomes bespottyd.
The last labor: the heavens with unbended
healse he bær, and eftsones for mede
the heavens deserued of the last labor.
Gaþ nu dyhtge menn hwider þe heye way
of grete ensample ledeþ! Hwy idlu
baks do you tourne? Þe erþe ouercomen
                yeldeþ the stars.

Liber v / Book v

I

Rupis Achaemeniae scopulis ubi versa sequentum
    Pectoribus figit spicula pugna fugax,
Tigris et Euphrates uno se fonte resolvunt
    Et mox abiunctis dissociantur aquis.
Si coeant cursumque iterum revocentur in unum,
    Confluat alterni quod trahit unda vadi;
Convenient puppes et vulsi flumine trunci
    Mixtaque fortuitos implicet unda modos,
Quos tamen ipsa vagos terrae declivia casus
    Gurgitis et lapsi defluus ordo regit.
Sic quae permissis fluitare videtur habenis
    Fors patitur frenos ipsaque lege meat.

["*Providence," says Boethius, "I understand from my own experience. But is there no such thing as chance?" "Yes—but not in the sense of randomness." Aristotle describes chance as an unintended outcome—as when a farmer in tilling his field finds gold. Chance, then, is an unexpected event resulting from the confluence of causes that, though unseen, exist nevertheless.*]

I

In þe kragges of Achaemenian cliffs where the warrior fleynge
    ficciþ arwes in his pursuers' breſtz,
þær ġe Tigris ġe Euphrates springaþ of anum wielle—
    and soone ben i-sundred in dyuerse watres.
If they meet again in one cours reclaimed,
    conflows in the currant what eache depthe hath drawen;
pouppes converge in þe flod eek ſtokkes araced,
    þa ſtreamas ġemenged tangell þing fortunel—
yet the shelvings of the erthe themselves and wæterġefealla
    wandryng happes þe slidyng ordre rewleþ.
Þus chaunce þat semeþ to flowe mid wealdleþrum
    aloose, it suffriþ bridelis and yemeþ hir lawe.

II

"*Pant ephoran kai pant epakouein*"
Puro clarum lumine Phoebum
Melliflui canit oris Homerus;
Qui tamen intima viscera terrae
Non valet aut pelagi radiorum
Infirma perrumpere luce.
Haud sic magni conditor orbis;
Huic ex alto cuncta tuenti
Nulla terrae mole resistunt,
Non nox atris nubibus obstat.
Quae sint, quae fuerint veniantque
Uno mentis cernit in ictu;
Quem, quia respicit omnia solus,
Verum possis dicere solem.

["I understand what you say," Boethius agrees, "but in this chain of causes is there no free will?" "Certainly," Philosophy replies, "otherwise there could be no such thing as a rational being." The greatest freedom is achieved in observing the divine mind; the least in choosing to become a slave of the body's wants. Free will itself, it would appear, is not spread evenly among humanity. Providence, looking down from eternity, doles out predetermined allotments according to merit.]

II

"He siehþ and he ġehierþ ealle þing"
of cleer Phoebus wiþ his pure lyght
sings þe hony mouþe of Homer.
Naþeles the deepest bowels of earth
and sea by þe bemes of hys wan
lemyng ne may he nat percen thurgh.
Not so of the great world its sċieppend
scanning ġesċeafta from on heye
gainst whom no waights of earth wiþstondaþ
ne niht mid hire miercum wolcnum.
What is, what was, and what shal bifall
in oo strook of mode he onġiett;
who soleyne þurhsiehþ ealle þing
him soþely þou maist clepe sol.

III

Quaenam discors foedera rerum
Causa resolvit? Quis tanta deus
Veris statuit bella duobus,
Ut quae carptim singula constent
Eadem nolint mixta iugari?
An nulla est discordia veris
Semperque sibi certa cohaerent,
Sed mens caecis obruta membris
Nequit oppressi lumnis igne
Rerum tenues noscere nexus?
Sed cur tanto flagrat amore
Veri tectas reperire notas?
Scitne quod appetit anxia nosse?

["I am still confused," says Boethius. "How can there be free
will when God foresees everything?" He dismisses as specious
the idea that God sees all future possibilities though only ne-
cessities in fact happen. This implies that divine providence is
subordinate to everyday matters, which cannot be so. Without
free will there can be no hope, no use for prayer, and human-
kind, as Philosophy has said, would be rent to pieces cut off
from its wellspring.]

III

What discordable cause þa sibbe
eallra þinga rends? Whiche god swich
werres sets betwix soþnessum twæm,
þat what singuler on styċċum standaþ
the selfsame mixt ne wolen nat been joined?
Or rather twixt trothes is there no discord
and æfre fæste þei cleuen to hem self,
but thoght confounded by blindid corse
ne may nat by fir of his flame opprest
wite þe þinne webb of þinges?
But why eschaufiþ it with suche desire
to find the secret signs of soþenesse?
Woot it what it secþ anxiously to know?

Sed quis nota scire laborat?
At si nescit, quid caeca petit?
Quis enim quidquam nescius optet
Aut quis valeat nescita sequi?
Quove inveniat, quisque repertam
Queat ignarus noscere formam?
An cum mentem cerneret altam,
Pariter summam et singula norat?
Nunc membrorum condita nube
Non in totum est oblita sui
Summamque tenet singula perdens.
Igitur quisquis vera requirit,
Neutro est habitu; nam neque novit
Nec penitus tamen omnia nescit,
Sed quam retinens meminit summam
Consulit alte visa retractans,
Ut servatis queat oblitas
       Addere partes.

Bot who trauileþ knowen þing to wit?
Yif he ne knoweþ nat, hu secþ he blind?
And certys who unknowyng wisceth for oght
or who may folwen þing þat ne beon knowen?
Oþþe hwær fint he him, and hwa unwis
mæġ þæt ġesċeap knowe whan yfounde?
Weere he þe heye thoght to byholde,
þan knoweþ he even þe somme and smal?
Now wiþdrawe in the clowd of body lymms
mod ne eallunga hine selfne forġeat
but holdeþ þe somme and lesiþ þe smal.
Lo whoever sekeþ soþenesse
nis in nouþir habit; he ne woot nat
alle depe, naþeles ne noot nat,
but what retaining remembriþ þe somme,
bythinketh apparence ysein on heye,
so that he may to the partz he kept
                join the partz forgot.

IV

Quondam porticus attulit
Obscuros nimium senes
Qui sensus et imagines
E corporibus extimis
Credant mentibus imprimi,
Ut quondam celeri stilo
Mos est aequore paginae,
Quae nullus habeat notas,
Pressas figere litteras.
Sed mens si propriis vigens
Nihil motibus explicat,
Sed tantum patiens iacet

["That is an ancient dispute," says Philosophy, "confounding the simplicity of divine prescience with humankind's notion of free will." Foreknowledge merely signifies the necessity of future occurrences but not their outcome. Boethius sees this as a contradiction because of his limited perception; after all, one's understanding of anything results from one's own powers, not those of the thing understood.]

IV

The Stoa brouhte ġear-dagum
ealde witan ful obscure
who the senses and ymages
fro bodies wiþouteforþe
believed in mens mindz ingrauen,
as at times wiþ swyfte poyntel
we ben wont on writbeċ leafe
þe næfþ næniġu ġewritu
to ficchen lettres emprentid.
Ac ġif þæt hwæte mod nanþing
ne arecþ by his awne wey,
only lieþ sufferantly
subgit to þo bodyes imprent

Notis subdita corporum
Cassasque in speculi vicem
Rerum reddit imagines,
Unde haec sic animis viget
Cernens omnia notio?
Quae vis singula perspicit
Aut quae cognita dividit?
Quae divisa recolligit
Alternumque legens iter
Nunc summis caput inserit,
Nunc decedit in infima,
Tum sese referens sibi
Veris falsa redarguit?
Haec est efficiens magis
Longe causa potentior
Quam quae materiae modo
Impressas patitur notas.
Praecedit tamen excitans
Ac vires animi movens
Vivo in corpore passio.
Cum vel lux oculos ferit
Vel vox auribus instrepit,
Tum mentis vigor excitus
Quas intus species tenet
Ad motus similes vocans
Notis applicat exteris
Introrsumque reconditis
Formis miscet imagines.

and right as a showglass yeldeþ
of mater veyne ymages,
whennes þus þe soules knowyng
þat þriuep and discerniþ al?
What power the partz byholdeþ,
and what the knowen þing deuides?
What þe þing deuided gadreþ
and chesyng entrechaunged path
now his heed lifteþ onlofte,
nu niþerweardes discendiþ,
than repeyring in to hym self
fals þing repreuiþ be trewe?
Þis is cause efficient
and of myght so mochel more
than suche as on mater only
suffriþ figures impressed.
Yet an affect in the quike
cors goþ byforne exciting
and moeuyng al so the myndz fors.
Whan ether light the yees doth smite
or voys hurtliþ to þe eres,
than the myndz strengh thus imoeuid
þe formes hit halt wiþynne,
clepyng þe semblable mocyouns,
ficciþ to þe figures ut
and wiþ þilke formes inne
medleþ utterest ymages.

V

Quam variis terras animalia permeant figuris!
Namque alia extento sunt corpore pulveremque verrunt
Continuumque trahunt vi pectoribus incitata sulcum,
Sunt quibus alarum levitas vaga verberetque ventos
Et liquido longi spatia aetheris enatet volatu,
Haec pressisse solo vestigia gressibusque gaudent
Vel virides campos transmittere vel subire silvas.
Quae variis videas licet omnia discrepare formis,
Prona tamen facies hebetes valet ingravare sensus.
Unica gens hominum celsum levat altius cacumen
Atque levis recto stat corpore despicitque terras.

["Knowledge is of various kinds," says Philosophy, "ordered
from the mere sensation of immovable creatures, such as mol-
lusks; to the imagination of animals that move, ever search-
ing; to human reason; to divine intelligence." The higher sub-
sume the lower. How can sense argue against imagination?
imagination against reason? reason against intelligence, or
foreknowledge infinite and pure?]

V

Hwæt, þa deor in divers hewes on erþe glyden!
For somme han hir bodies straught and swapaþ dust,
with fors of brest afysed, dragaþ singal spor;
oþere beat the winds wiþ wenges light and free
and swim in flight thorow liquid spaces of þe longe eyre;
þo gladen hem to sette her traas on ground, on foot
or griny fildz to pas or walken under waldes.
Thogh alle discorden by dyuerse formes you see,
yet faces held ofdune heuieþ dullid sencis.
Manncynn ana heueþ heyer hys eye heued,
at ease doth stand wiþ body vpryht, ofersiehþ þa eorþan.
This figure warns, unles þu dwæsast, ofereorþfæst,

Haec nisi terrenus male desipis, admonet figura,
Qui recto caelum vultu petis exserisque frontem,
In sublime feras animum quoque, ne gravata pessum
Inferior sidat mens corpore celsius levato.

with lifted looke aspiring, þi frount to heuene-ward,
mod eac on heahnesse ahefe! þy læs grundlunga
thy mynd niþor sitte, thy cors leved aloft.

["If *understanding results from one's own nature," Philoso-
phy continues, "what then can we comprehend of God's
understanding of things?" God is eternal. He perceives the
limitless universe, past and future time, in the infinite present.
From this perspective, all occurrences are concurrent, with this
distinction: out of pure necessity, the sun must rise and set;
while a man may (or may not) go walking, out of condi-
tional necessity—the condition being his own ability and
choice of action. And the greatest necessity, Philosophy con-
cludes, is this: "Wel to don afore the eyes of þe iuge þat seeþ
alle."]*

"While Boethius, oppressed with fetters, expected each moment the sentence or the stroke of death, he composed in the tower of Pavia the *Consolation of Philosophy*.... Suspense, the worst of evils, was at length determined by the ministers of death, who executed, and perhaps exceeded, the inhuman mandate of Theodoric. A strong cord was fastened round the head of Boethius, and forcibly tightened till his eyes almost started from their sockets; and some mercy may be discovered in the milder torture of beating him with clubs till he expired."

—EDWARD GIBBON

GLOSSARY

The entries in this glossary include proper names and words used in the text of the translation that are not part of the familiar vocabulary of contemporary English. Following the main entry, the etymology of the word is given; its meaning or meanings in the present context; and the variant forms or peculiar phrases in which it is employed, identified where relevant by gender, case, and number, or person, tense, mood, and number. In general, parts of speech are not indicated, and grammatical gender (limited in English to pronouns and additionally in Old English to nouns and adjectives) only where it seems necessary.

ABBREVIATIONS

ac., accusative

adj., adjective

adv., adverb

dat., dative

dem., demonstrative

fem., feminine

gen., genitive

imp., imperative

inf., infinitive

infl., inflected

L, Latin

masc., masculine

ME, Middle English

N., Northern

neut., neuter

Obs., Obsolete (late 15th through
18th centuries)

OE, Old English

p., past

pres. pt., present participle

p. pt., past participle

pl., plural

pres., present

sing., singular

subj., subjunctive

A A (OE) always, forever. Phrases: NE...A, never.

ABLYNG (ME) enabling (*pres. pt.*).

ABRÆDEN (OE) to open out, stretch.

ACAST (ME, Obs.) to throw down.

ACENNAN (OE) to bear a child. Forms: ACENNED, *p. pt.*

ACHAEMENIAN, Persian, referring to Achaemenes, founder of an ancient dynasty.

ACHEESEN (ME) to choose out, select.

ACHELOUS (L) river in ancient Greece, whose god in the form of a bull fought with Hercules, who broke off one his horns.

ACHOKEN (ME) to choke. Forms: ACHEKED, *p. pt.*

AĊIERRAN (OE) to turn. Forms: AĊIERRED, *p. pt.*

ACLEOFAN (OE) to cleave, split. Forms: ACLEAF, *3 p. sing.*

ACWELLAN (OE) to destroy, kill. Forms: ACWEALDE, *3 p. sing.*

ADOUN (ME) down.

ADREDAN (ME) to dread, fear. Forms: ADREDE, *3 pres. pl.*

ADRÆFEN (OE) to drive off, expel. Forms: ADRÆFÞ, *3 pres. sing.*

Æ (OE) law. Forms: —, *ac. sing., gen. sing.*

ÆCER (OE) acre, field. Forms: ÆCERA, *gen. pl.*

ÆFENSĊUWA (OE) evening shadow. Forms: ÆFEN-SĊUWAN, *ac. pl.*

ÆFTER (OE) after.

ÆFTERCWEÞAN (OE) to speak afterward. Forms: ÆFTERCWIÞÞ, *3 pres. sing.*

ÆR (OE) before, previously.

ÆROR (OE) previously (*adv.*).

ÆRRA (OE) former. Forms: ÆRRAN, *masc. nom. sing.*; ÆRRE, *fem. nom. sing.*

ÆTGÆDERE (OE) together.

ÆÞELE (OE) noble.

ÆWELM (OE) fountain, spring.

AFFRIKE (ME) Africa.

AFLIEGAN (OE) to put to flight.

AFLIGHT (ME) afflicted.

AFORE (Obs.) before.

AFYSAN (OE) to incite, impel. Forms: AFYSED, *p. pt.*

AGASTE (ME) to terrify. Forms: AGAST, *p. pt.*

AGEN (OE) own. Forms: AGENE, *masc. ac. pl.*

AGE(I)(Y)N(E) (ME) again.

AHEBBAN (OE) to lift up. Forms: AHEFE, *imp. sing.*

AKNOWEN (ME) to perceive, recognize.

AL (ME) entirely.

AL (ME, Obs.) all.

ALIESAN (OE) to release. Forms: ALIESEÞ, *3 pres.sing.*; ALIESAÞ, *3 pres. pl.*

ALLE (ME) all.

ALLYEN (ME) to make an alliance, unite. Forms: ALLYED, *p. pt.*

ALOOSE (Obs.) loose, slack.

ALS (ME) also.

ALSWA (ME) also, too.

ALÞERBESTE (ME) best of all.

ALÞERFAIREST (ME) fairest of all.

AN (OE) one. Forms: ANUM, *masc. dat.*

AN (Obs.) if.

ANA (OE) alone, only.

ANPÆÞ (OE) narrow path.

ANOIOUS (ME) hurtful.

ANTAEUS (L) Libyan giant, killed by Hercules.

APAYED (ME) satisfied.

APPARENCE (ME) appearance.

ARACE (ME) to uproot. Forms: ARACED, *p. pt.*

ARCTURUS (L) brightest star in the northern constellation Boötes.

ARISAN (OE) to arise, rise. Forms: ARIST, *3 pres. sing.*

AR(I)(Y)S(I)(Y)NG(E) (ME) rising.

ARMES (Obs.) arms, armies.

ARMONIE (Obs.) concord, harmony.

AREĊĊAN (OE) to explain. Forms: ARECÞ, *3 pres. sing.*

ARWE (ME) arrow. Forms: ARWES, *pl.*

ARWORTHY (Obs.) honorable, reverend.

ASCENDEN (ME) to ascend. Forms: ASCENDE, *pres. subj. sing.*

ASĊINAN (OE) to shine forth. Forms: ASĊINAÞ, *3 pres. pl.*

ASĊRINCAN (OE) to shrink. Forms: ASĊRINCÞ, *3 pres. sing.*

ASMOCHE (Obs.) as much.

ASTONIED (ME, Obs.) bewildered, dazed, stunned.

ASTYRIAN (OE) to agitate, move, stir. Forms: ASTYREST, *2 pres. sing.*

ATEMIAN (OE) to tame.

ATTEMPERAUNCE (ME) tempering.

ATTEMPRE (ME) to moderate, temper. Forms: ATTEMPREÞ, *3 pres. sing.*

ATRIDES (L) literally, "son of Atreus"—i. e., Agamemnon, legendary king of Mycenae who led the Greek forces in the Trojan War.

AULIXES (OE, L) Ulysses, Odysseus in Greek, hero of the *Odyssey* of Homer.

AUNCIENT (Obs.) ancient.

AUTUMPNE (ME) autumn.

AWEĊĊAN (OE) to awaken, excite. Forms: AWEHT, *p. pt.*

AWNE (ME) own.

AXEN (ME) to ask. Forms: AXED, *p. pt.*

AXILL (Obs.) turning wheel.

AY (ME) ever.

AYEIN (ME) again.

AYWHERE (Obs.) everywhere.

B   BAK (Obs.) back. Forms: BAKS, *pl.*

BALOCRÆFT (OE) evil craft, magic. Forms: BALO-CRÆFTUM, *dat. pl.*

BAN (OE) bone. Forms:—, *ac. pl.*

BAR (OE) boar. Forms: BARES, *gen. sing.*

BATAILE (ME) battle.

BEAUTEE (ME) beauty.

BE (ME) by.

BEAR, the northern constellation Ursa Major.

BEEM (ME) beam, ray. Forms: BEMES, *pl.*

BE(E)N(E) (ME) to be. Forms: BESE, *3 pres. sing.* (N. dialect); BEN, *pres. pl.*; WEERE, *3 p. subj. sing.*; BEN, *p. pt.*

BEERE (ME) bear.

BEGYNNYNG (ME) beginning. Forms: BEGYNNYNGES, *pl.*

BEHEALDAN (OE) to behold, possess. Forms: BEHIELT, *3 pres. sing.*; BEHEALD, *imp. sing.*

BEND (OE) bond, chain. Forms: BENDAS, *ac. pl.*

BEON (OE) to be. Forms: BEOÞ, SINT, *3 pres. pl.*

BERAN (OE) to bear. Forms: BERAÞ, *3 pres. pl.*; BÆR, *3 p. sing.*

BERE(N) (ME) to bear, carry. Forms: BERIÞ, *3 pres. sing.*; BERYNG, *pres. pt.*

BERERE (ME) bearer.

BESENĊAN (OE) to sink, submerge. Forms: BESENĊED, *p. pt.*

BESINES (ME) attention, care.

BESPOTTEN (ME) to stain. Forms: BESPOTTYD, *3 p. sing.*

BESTOWNE (Obs.) bestowed.

BEWTIX (OE) between.

BEWÆPNIAN (OE) to disarm. Forms: BEWÆPNAST, *2 pres. sing.*

BEWET (ME, Obs.) to wet thoroughly. Forms:—, *p. pt.*

BEWRIÞAN (OE) to bind around, envelop. Forms: BEWRIÞÞ, *3 pres. sing.*

BIDDAN (OE) to pray. Forms: BÆD, *3 p. sing.*

BIFALL (Obs.) to come about, happen.

BIFOULET (ME) befouled.

BINDAN (OE) to bind. Forms: BINTST, *2 pres. sing.*; BINDEÞ, *3 pres. sing.*

BIRDZ (Obs.) birds, *pl.*

BIRHTU (OE) brightness. Forms:—, *ac. sing.*

BISET (Obs.) to beset. Forms: BISETZ, *3 pres. sing.*

BISPELL (OE) parable, story.

BIWAILE (ME) to bewail.

BLANDAN (OE) to blend, infect, mix. Forms: ĠEBLANDEN, *p. pt.*

BLAUNDISSYNG (ME) blandishing.

BLENDEN (ME) to blend. Forms: BLENDE, *p. pt.*

BLETSIAN (OE) to bless. Forms: BLEDSODE, *3 p. sing.*

BLINDE (ME) blind.

BLINDID (Obs.) blind, blinded.

BL(I)(Y)SFUL (ME) blissful, happy.

BLIÞE (OE) gentle, happy, kind. Forms: BLIÞNE, *ac. sing.*

BLIÞOR (OE) happier, more gladly, more pleasantly.

BLOD (OE) blood. Forms: BLODE, *dat. sing.*

BLODDRYNCE (OE) bloodshed. Forms:—, *dat. sing.*

BLODY (ME) bloody.

BLOSTM (OE) blossom, flower. Forms: BLOSTMA, *gen. pl.*

BLOWE (ME) to blow. Forms: BLEWH, *3 pres. sing.*

BODIAN (OE) to announce, proclaim. Forms: BODAÞ, *3 pres. sing.*

BODYES (ME) bodies' (*gen. pl.*).

BOETES (ME, L) the northern constellation Boötes, "the ox-driver."

BONDIS (ME) bonds, chains, *pl.*

BONDZ (Obs.) bonds, *pl.*

BOORE (ME) boar.

BOREAS (L) the north wind.

BOT (ME) but.

BOTME (ME) bottom.

BRAD (OE) broad. Forms: BRADE, *masc. ac. pl.*

BRÆÞ (OE) exhalation.

BRAUNCHE (ME) branch. Forms: BRAUNCHES, *pl.*

BRENK (ME) riverbank, shore.

BRENNE (ME) to burn. Forms: BRENNEÞ, *3 pres. sing.*

BREOST (OE) chest, mind. Forms:—, *ac. pl.*

BREOSTHORD (OE) heart's depth. Forms: BREOST-HORDE, *dat. sing.*

BREST (Obs.) breast, chest. Forms: BRESTZ, *pl.*

BR(I)(Y)D (ME) bird.

BRIDEL (ME) bridle. Forms: BRIDEL(E)(I)S, *pl.*

BRINGAN (OE) to bring, bring forth. Forms: BROHT, *p. pt.*

BRINGEN (ME) to bring, introduce. Forms: BROUHTE, 3
pres. sing.

BRINNE (ME) to burn. Forms: BRYNYD, 3 p. sing.

BROC (OE) brook.

BROÞER (ME) brother.

BROÐOR (OE) brother. Forms:—, gen. sing.

BRUTUS (L) Marcus Junius Brutus (d. 42 B.C.), Roman
senator and assassin of Julius Caesar.

BRYDBUR (OE) bridal chamber.

BRYHTNES (ME) brightness, splendor.

BRYNGEN (ME) to bring. Forms: BROWT, p. pt.

BUFAN (OE) above.

BURÞE (ME) birth, origin.

BY CAUSE (ME) because.

BYCGAN (OE) to buy. Forms: BOHTE, 3 p. sing.

BYDE (ME) to remain. Forms: BYDEN, pres. pl.

BYFORNE (ME) before.

BYHOLDE (ME) to behold, see. Forms: BYHOLDEÞ, 3 pres.
sing.

BYSEGEN (ME) to besiege. Forms: BYSEGED, p. pt.

BYTHINKEN (ME) to consider. Forms: BYTHINKETH, 3
pres. sing.

CACCHEN (ME) to catch, take captive. Forms: YCAUGHT,   C
p. pt.

CACUS (L) three-headed giant who tried to rob Hercules
of the cattle he had stolen from the monster
Geryon.

CALME (ME) calm.

CANCER (L) the constellation Cancer ("Crab"), into
    which the sun enters at midsummer.

CARKE (Obs.) effort, toil.

CASTEN (ME) to throw. Forms: CASTE, *p. pt.*

CATON (ME, L) Marcus Porcius Cato "the Younger" (d.
    46 B.C.), Roman senator noted for his Stoicism
    and severity.

ĊEALD (OE) cold. Forms:—, *nom. sing.*

CENTAURIS (L, ME) *pl.*, the Centaurs, a Thessalian tribe
    of monsters, half man, half horse, conquered by
    Hercules.

CEPTRE (ME) scepter.

CERBERUS (L), three-headed dog that guarded the Un-
    derworld.

CERCLE (ME) circle, orbit.

CERES (L) goddess of agriculture.

CERTA(E)YN(E) (ME) certain, fixed, sure.

CERT(E)(Y)S (ME) certainly.

CESSE(N) (ME) to cease, stop. Forms: CESEÞ, *3 pres. sing.*

CHACEN (ME) to harass. Forms: CHACEÞ, *3 pres. sing.*

CHARE (ME) chariot.

CHARGE (ME) to load. Forms:—, *pres. sing. subj.*

CHAUNCE (ME) chance, fortune.

CHAUNGEN (ME) to change. Forms: CHAUNGEÞ, *3 pres.
    sing.;* ICHAUNGED, *p. pt.*

CHAW (Obs.) jaw. Forms: CHAWES, *pl.*

CHAYER (ME) chair. Forms: CHAYERS, *pl.*

CHEKE (ME) cheek. Forms: CHEKES, *pl.*

CHERE (ME) face.

CHESEN (ME) to choose. Forms: CHESYNG, *pres. pt.*

CHEYNE (ME) chain.

CHIRKYNGE (ME) groaning.

CLARIOUN (ME) clarion, trumpet. Forms: CLARIOUNS, *pl.*

CLAWE (ME) claw.

CLEPE (ME) to call, name. Forms: CLEPYNG, *pres. pt.*

CLE(E)R(E) (ME) bright, clear, pure.

CLIVEN (ME) to cling. Forms: CLYUETH, *3 pres. sing.*;
        CLEUEN, *3 pres. pl.*

CLOÞEN (ME) to clothe, dress. Forms: CLOÞED, *p. pt.*

CLOWD (ME) cloud.

COMEN (ME) to come. Forms: COMTH, *3 pres. sing.*

COMMOEVE (ME) to influence, move. Forms: COM-
        MOEVYNG, *pres. pt.*

COMPAS (ME) circuit.

CONFLOW (Obs.) to flow together. Forms: CONFLOWS,
        3 pres. sing.

CONFOUNDEN (ME) to overwhelm. Forms: CON-
        FOUNDED, *p. pt.*

CONNE (ME) to know, understand. Forms: CON, *imp.*

COPP (OE) summit, top.

CORAGE (ME) heart, spirit. Forms: CORAGES, *pl.*

CORNES (ME) grain crops, *pl.*

CORS (ME) body.

CORSE (Obs.) body.

COUERE (ME) to cover. Forms: YCOUERED, *p. pt.*

COURS (ME) course.

COUÞ (ME) known.

COVETOUR (ME) covetous person.

CRAKE (Obs.) to boast.

CROPP (ME) tip, top.

CRUDAN (OE) to press. Forms: CRUDAÞ, *3 pres. pl.*

CRUELL (ME) cruel.

CRUELTE (ME) cruelty.

CURE (ME) attention, care.

CURRANT (Obs.) current.

CWIC (OE) alive, living, quick. Forms: CWICNE, *masc. ac. sing.*

CYNING (OE) king.

CYST (OE) the choicest.

D DÆL (OE) part. Forms: DÆLUM, *dat. pl.*

DARTE (ME) spear. Forms: DARTES, *pl.*

DEAD (OE) dead. Forms: DEADNE, *masc. ac. sing.*

DEAÞ (OE) death. Forms:—, *ac. sing.*

DEBONAIR (ME) gentle, submissive.

DEDDE (Obs.) extinguished.

DEEÞ (ME) death.

DEFOULEN (ME) to disfigure. Forms: DEFOWLED, *p. pt.*

DELVEN (ME) to dig. Forms: DALF, *3 p. sing.*

DEMEN (ME) to distinguish. judge. Forms:—, *3 pres. pl.*

DEOP (OE) deep. Forms:—, *neut. ac. sing.*

DEOPE (OE) deep *(adv.)*.

DEOR (OE) animal. Forms:—, *pl.*

DEPE (ME) deeply.

DEPTHE (Obs.) depth.

DERK (ME) dark.

DERKNESSE (ME) darkness. Forms: DERKNESSES, *pl.*

DESARTZ (Obs.) deserts.

DESCOUEREN (ME) to disclose, reveal, uncover. Forms:
 DESCOUEREÞ, *3 pres. sing.*

DESERUE (ME) to deserve, merit. Forms: DESERUED, *3 p.
 sing.*

DESIAR (Obs.) desire.

DESIJRE (ME) desire. Forms: DESIJRES, *pl.*

DESPIT (ME) envy, spite.

DEUIDE (Obs.) to divide. Forms: DEUIDES, *3 pres. sing.*;
 DEUIDED, *p. pt.*

DEWE (ME) deserved, just.

DEYE (ME) dye.

DISCENDE (ME) to descend, go down. Forms: DISCEN-
 DIÞ, *3 pres. sing.*

DISCERNE (ME) to discern. Forms: DISCERNIÞ, *3 pres. sing.*

DISCHE (Obs.) dish.

DISCORDE (ME) to disagree. Forms: DISCORDEN, *3 pres.
 sing.*

DISCORDABLE (ME) discordant.

DISCORDAUNT (ME) discordant, dissonant.

DISCOURS (Obs.) process, reasoning.

DISPISEN (ME) to scorn, despise. Forms: DISPISEÞ, *3 pres.
 sing.*

DIVERS (Obs.) diverse, various.

DOGHTER (ME) daughter. Forms:—, *gen. sing.*

DON (OE) to do.

DOON (ME) to do. Forms: DOOTH, *3 pres. sing.*

DOUBLEN (ME) to double. Forms: DOUBELYTH, *3 pres. sing.*

DOUNE (ME) down.

DRAGAN (OE) to drag, draw. Forms: DRAGAÞ, *3 pres. sing.*

DRAGOUN (ME) dragon, serpent.

DRAWE (ME) to carry along, drag, draw. Forms: DRAWETH, *3 pres. sing.*; DRAWE, *3 pres. pl.*; DROUGH, *3 p. sing.*; DRAWEN, *p. pt.*;

DREDFULL (Obs.) dreadful.

DREDLES (ME) without fear.

DRENCHEN (ME) to drawn, overwhelm. Forms: DREYNT, *p. pt.*

DRERY (ME) sad.

DRYGAN (OE) to dry. Forms: DRYGEÞ, *3 pres. sing.*

DRYĠE (OE) dry land. Forms:—, *dat. sing.*

DRYĠE (OE) dry. Forms:—, *masc. nom. sing.*

DRYNKE (ME) drink.

DUC (ME) duke.

DULCE (Obs.) dulcet, sweet.

DULLID (Obs.) dulled.

DWÆSIAN (OE) to be foolish, become stupid. Forms: DWÆSAST, *2 pres. sing.*

DWELLEN (ME) to remain. Forms: DWELLIÞ, *3 pres. sing.*

DYHTIĠ (OE) strong. Forms: DYHTĠE, *masc. nom. pl.*

DYOMED (L, ME) king of Thrace who owned a herd of flesh-eating mares; killed and fed to his horses by Hercules.

DYSIĠ (OE) foolish. Forms: DYSIĠA, *masc. nom. sing.*

DYUERSE (ME) diverse.

EA (OE) river. Forms:—, gen. sing.　　　　Є

EAC (OE) also.

EACHE (Obs.) each.

EALA (OE) alas.

EALD (OE) old. Forms: EALDE, masc. ac. pl.

EALL (OE) all. Forms: EALLES, gen. sing.; EALLE, neut. ac.
　　　pl.; EALLRA, neut. gen. pl.

EALLUNGA (OE) entirely.

EALLWIHTA (OE) all creatures. Forms:—, ac. pl.

ECE (OE) eternal.

E(E)K(E) (ME, Obs.) also.

EFNE (OE) even, just; justly.

EFT (OE, ME) afterward.

EFTSONES (ME) in return.

EGRE (ME) bitter, sharp.

E(I)(Y)R(E) (ME) air.

ELDE (ME) old age.

ELEMENTZ (Obs.) elements.

ELLYS (ME)　else, otherwise.

ELZ (Obs.) else.

EMPRENTID (ME) imprinted.

ENDE (OE) end.

END(E) (ME) limit, purpose.

ENDITEN (ME) to dictate, write. Forms: ENDITETH, 3
　　　pres. sing.

ENDSET (OE) final sunset. Forms: ENDSETE, dat. sing.

ENSAMPLE (ME) example.

ENSPIRE (ME) to breathe forth. Forms: ENSPIREÞ, *3 pres. sing.*

ENTERCHAUNGYNG (ME) exchanging.

ENTRECHAUNGEN (ME) to alternate, exchange, interchange, reverse. Forms: ENTRECHAUNGEÞ, *3 pres. sing.*; ENTERCHAUNGYNG, *pres. pt.*; ENTRECHAUNGED, *p. pt.*

ENTRECHAUNGING (ME) reversal. Forms: ENTRECHAUNGINGES, *pl.*

ENTRELACED (ME) intermingled.

ENUYROND (Obs.) surrounded.

EORÞE (OE) earth. Forms: EORÞAN, *ac. sing., gen. sing.*

EQUITE (ME) equity, justice.

ERE (ME) ear. Forms: EARS, *pl.*

ERTHE (Obs.) earth.

ERÞE (ME) earth, world.

ERÞELY (ME) earthly.

ESCHAUFEN (ME) to burn, heat. Forms: ESCHAUF(E)(I)Þ, *3 pres. sing.*

ESTAT (ME) condition, state.

ESTEWYNDE (ME) east wind.

EÞEL (OE) native country.

ETHER (Obs.) either.

EUESTERRE (ME) evening star.

EUENE (ME) evening.

EUENLYK (ME) identical.

EUPHRATES (L) with the Tigris, one of the two chief rivers of Mesopotamia.

EURIPUS (L) the turbulent strait between Euboea and
    Boeotia.

EURUS (L) the east or southeast wind.

EURYDICE (L) wife of Orpheus.

EVANDER (L) Italian king in whose region lived the rob-
    ber Cacus.

EVEN (ME) equally.

EYEN (ME) eyes, *pl.*

EYÞER (ME) each, either.

FABRICIUS (L) Gaius Fabricius Luscinus (d. 250 B.C.),   F
    Roman general and consul of fabled virtue.

FÆDER (OE) father. Forms:—, *ac. sing.*

FÆST (OE) fast, firm. Forms: FÆSTE, *fem. ac. sing.*; FÆST,
    fem. nom. pl.

FÆSTE (OE) firmly.

FA(I)(Y)RE (ME, Obs.) fair, fine, orderly.

FAL (Obs.) to fall. Forms: FALZ, *3 pres. sing.*

FALLEN (ME) to fall, to happen. Forms: FALLEÞ, *3 pres.
    sing.*; YFALLE, *p. pt.*

FALS (ME) deceptive, false.

FALZ (Obs.) false.

FARAN (OE) to travel. Forms: FARE, *pres. subj. sing.*

FASOUN (ME) fabric, working order.

FAST (Obs.) tenacious.

FAUCHON (ME) billhook, sickle.

FEALLAN (OE) to fall. Forms: FEOLL, *3 pres. sing.*

FEARN (OE) fern. Forms:—, *ac. pl.*

FEBLE (ME) weak.

FEDAN (OE) to feed, nourish. Forms: FETT, *3 pres. sing.*;
       FEDE, *pres. sing. subj.*

FEDEN (ME) to feed. Forms: FEDDE, *3 p. sing.*

FEERE (ME) fear.

FEIÞ (ME) trust.

FELA (OE) many.

FELAWE (ME) companion, friend. Forms: FELAWES, *pl.*

FELDE (ME) field.

FELEN (ME) to find out, perceive. Forms:—, *pres. pl.*

FELL(E) (ME) fierce.

FELOWN (ME) criminal. Forms: FELOWNES, *gen. sing.*;
       FELOWNS, *pl.*

FEOH (OE) money, property.

FEORR (OE) far, distant.

FERE (ME) companion, friend, mate.

FERNE (ME) distant, remote.

FERREST (ME) farthest.

FERUENT (Obs.) fervent, glowing.

FERVENTAR (Obs.) feverish.

FETER (OE) fetter. Forms: FETERUM, *dat. pl.*

FEÞER (OE) feather, (*pl.*) wings. Forms: FEÞERA, *ac. pl.*

FERSERE (ME) fiercer.

FFOLKE (Obs.) folk, people.

FICCHEN (ME) to affx. Forms: FICCIÞ, *3 pres. sing.*

FIERS (Obs.) fierce.

FIL (Obs.) to fill.

FILDZ (Obs.) fields (*pl.*).

FINDAN (OE) to find. Forms: FINT, *3 pres. sing.*

FINDEN (ME) to find, discover. Forms: YFOUNDE, *p. pt.*

FIR (ME) fire.

FISĊ (OE) fish. Forms: FISĊAS, *nom. pl.*

FISCHE (Obs.) fish.

FLEA (Obs.) to flay. Forms: FLEAD, *3 p. sing.*

FLEEN (ME) to flee. Forms: FLEYNGE, *pres. pt.*

FLEMEN (ME) to banish. Forms: FLEME, *imp. sing.*

FLETEN (ME) to float, flow.

FLITFULL (OE) contentious.

FLITTE (ME) to move. Forms: YFLIT, *p. pt.*

FLODWIELM (OE) agitated waters.

FLO(O)D (ME) flood. Forms: FLOODES, *pl.*, waters.

FLORISHING (Obs.) showy.

FLOTERYNGE (ME) floating, unstable, *pres. pt.*

FLOWE (ME) to flow.

FODOR (OE) fodder. Forms: FODRE, *dat. sing.*

FOLWEN (ME) to follow, pursue.

FORBERSTAN (OE) to break. Forms: FORBORSTENUM,
     p. pt. masc. dat. sing. & pl.

FORBURN (Obs.) to destroy with fire. Forms: FORBRENT,
     p. pt.

FORDOON (ME) to destroy.

FOREYN(E) (ME) foreign, strange.

FORĠIETAN (OE) to forget. Forms: FORĠEAT, *3 p. sing.*

FORĠIETOL (OE) forgetful.

FORHEED (ME) forehead.

FORHYDAN (OE) to hide. Forms: FORHYDDE, *3 p. sing.*

FORLÆTAN (OE) to abandon, leave, relinquish. Forms:
     FORLÆT, *3 pres. sing.*; FORLÆTENNE, *masc. ac.
     sing. p. pt.*

FORLEOSAN (OE) to lose. Forms: FORLYST, *3 pres. sing.*;
     FORLEAS, *3 p. sing.*; FORLOREN, *p. pt.*

FORLETE (ME, Obs.) to abandon, leave. Forms:
     FORLETEÞ, *3 pres. sing.*; FORLETE, *p. pt.*

FORLOST (ME) destroyed, totally lost.

FORME (ME, Obs.) form, shape. Forms: FORMES, *pl.*

FORME-FADER (ME) ancestor, forefather. Forms:
     FORME-FADRES, *pl.*

FORS (ME, Obs.) force, power.

FORS (Obs.) to force. Forms: FORST, *3 pres. pl.*

FORSĊIEPPAN (OE) to transform. Forms: FORSĊIEPÞ,
     3 pres. sing.

FORSLES (Obs.) impotent, powerless.

FORSOÞ (OE) truly.

FORÞBÆRE (OE) productive. Forms: FORÞBÆRRAN, *neut.*
     ac. pl.

FORÞBERAN (OE) to produce. Forms: FORÞBIRST, *2 pres.*
     sing.; FORÞBIRÞ, *3 pres. sing.*

FORÞBRINGAN (OE) to bring forth, produce. Forms:
     FORÞBRINGÞ, *3 pres. sing.*

FORTUNEL (ME) fortuitous.

FORWEORÞAN (OE) to perish. Forms: FORWEARÞ, *3 p.*
     sing.

FORWHY (ME) wherefore, why.

FRAM (OE) from.

FREMSUM (OE) benign, kindly. Forms: FREMSUME, *fem.*
     ac. sing.

FREOSAN (OE) to freeze. Forms: FROREN, *p. pt.*

FRETEN (ME) to devour. Forms:—, p. pt.

FRIÞ (OE) truce.

FRO (ME) from.

FROUNT (ME) forehead.

FRUMA (OE) beginning. Forms: FRUMAN, dat. sing.

FRUYT (ME) fruit.

FUL (ME) completely, fully.

FULFILLE (ME) to fulfill.

FULLE (ME) to complete, fulfill.

FULLE (ME) full.

FULLFYLLING (ME, Obs.) fulfillment.

FYN (ME) end, limit.

FYR (OE) fire. Forms: FYRES, gen. sing.

FYRE (Obs.) fire.

FYRS (OE) furze. Forms: FYRSAS, ac. pl.

FYUE (ME) five.

GADER (ME) to gather. Forms: GADREÞ, 3 pres. sing.   **G**

GÆRS (OE) grass.

GAN (OE) to go. Forms: GÆÞ, 3 pres. sing.; GAÞ, imp. pl.

GAST (OE) spirit.

GAYNYNG (Obs.) gain, profit.

ĠE (OE) and. Phrases: ĠE...ĠE, both...and.

ĠEAR-DAGAS (OE) days of yore. Forms: ĠEAR-DAGUM,
    dat. pl.

ĠEATWEARD (OE) gatekeeper.

ĠEBINDAN (OE) to bind. Forms: ĠEBINDEÞ, 3 pres. sing.

ĠEBRINGAN (OE) to bring, bring forth. Forms:
    ĠEBRINGÞ, 3 pres. sing.

ĠEDON (OE) to do, make. Forms: ĠEDYDE, *3 p. sing.*

ĠEDWOLMIST (OE) mist of error. Forms: —, *nom. sing.*

ĠEEMNETTAN (OE) to make level, even. Forms: ĠEEMNETT, *3 pres. sing.*

(ĠE)GADRIAN (OE) to gather. Forms: ĠEGADRAST, *2 pres. sing.*; GADRIĠE, *pres. sing. subj.*

ĠEHIERAN (OE) to hear. Forms: ĠEHIERÞ, *3 pres. sing.*

ĠEMANG (OE) among.

ĠEMUNAN (OE) to remember. Forms: ĠEMAN, *3 pres. sing.*

ĠENOH (OE) enough.

ĠEOND (OE) throughout, as far as.

ĠERÆW (OE) row, succession.

ĠESĊEAFT (OE) creation, element. Forms: ĠESĊEAFTA, *nom. & ac. pl.*

ĠESĊEAP (OE) form, shape.

ĠES(E)(I)ON (OE) to see. Forms: ĠESIHST, *2 pres. sing.*; ĠESIEHÞ, *3 pres. sing.*

GEST (ME, Obs.) guest. Forms: GESTES, *pl.*; GESTZ, *gen. pl.*

ĠESUND (OE) healthy, sound. Forms: ĠESUNDNE, *ac. sing.*

GETEN (ME) to get.

ĠEÞWÆRE (OE) concordant, harmonious. Forms: ĠEÞWÆRUM, *masc. dat. pl.*

ĠEWEALDAN (OE) to rule. Forms: ĠEWIELT, *3 pres. sing.*

ĠEWRIT (OE) writing. Forms: ĠEWRITU, *ac. pl.*

GIDE (Obs.) to guide.

ĠIEFAN (OE) to give. Forms: ĠEAF, *3 pres. sing.*

ĠIF (OE) if.

GIN (Obs.) to begin. Forms:—, *imp. sing.*

GLADEN (ME) to rejoice. Forms:—, *3 pres. pl.*

GLADSOM (ME) pleasing.

GLÆDNES (OE) gladness. Forms: GLÆEDNESSE, *ac. sing.*

GLÆSHLUTTOR (OE) glassy clear, vitreous.

GLIW (OE) music. Forms: GLIWE, *dat. sing.*

GLYDE (Obs.) to glide.

GLYDEN (ME) to travel, traverse. Forms:—, *3 pres. pl.*

GNAWE (ME) to gnaw. Forms: GNAWYNG, *pres. pt.*

GOD (OE) good. Forms: GODES, *gen. sing.*; GODU, *ac. pl.*

GODDES (ME) goddess.

GON (ME) to go. Forms: GOÞ, *3 pres. sing.*

GODHED (ME) divinity.

GOLDENE (ME) golden.

GOLDHORD (OE) treasure. Forms: GOLDHORDE, *dat. sing.*

GOODZ (Obs.) goods.

GOUERNANCE (ME) control, rule.

GOVERNE (ME) to control, govern. Forms: GO-VERNYNGE, *pres. pt.*

GREKYSSHE (ME) Greek.

GRETE (ME) great.

GREVOUS (ME, Obs.) heavy, oppressive, painful.

GRIDY (Obs.) greedy.

GRIMM (OE) cruel, fierce. Forms: GRIMNE, *masc. ac. sing.*

GRINY (Obs.) greeny.

GRUNDLUNGA (OE) pulled down to the ground.

GRYM (ME) grim.

GRYPH (Obs.) vulture.

GRYRE (OE) terror.

 h̥ HABBAN (OE) to have. Forms: HÆBBE, *1 pres. sing.*; HÆFÞ,
   3 pres. sing.

HABIT (ME) condition, state.

HABOUNDE (ME) to abound. Forms: HABOUNDEN, *pres.*
   pl.

HÆRFEST (OE) autumn, harvest.

HÆTE (OE) heat. Forms:—, *dat. sing.*

HÆTO (OE) heat. Forms:—, *dat. sing.*

HAP (ME, Obs.) chance. Forms: HAPPES, *pl.* (ME).

HARDE (ME) hard, harsh.

HARSK (ME) rough.

HARME (ME) grief, ills, woe.

HART (Obs.) heart. Forms: HARTZ, *gen. sing., pl.*

HATAN (OE) to bid, command. Forms: HÆST, *2 pres. sing.*;
   HOTEN, *p. pt.*

HAUGHT (Obs.) haughty, high.

HAUTEYN (ME) haughty, proud.

HAUYNG (ME) owning.

HAVEN (ME) to have. Forms: HAT (var. of HATH), *3 pres.*
   sing.; HAÞ, *3 pres. sing.*; HAN, *3 pres. pl.*; HADDE,
   3 p. sing.

HEAH (OE) high. Forms: HEAN, *masc. gen. sing.*

HEAHCYNING (OE) high king. Forms: HEAHCYNINGAS,
   nom. & ac. pl.

HEAHMUNT (OE) high mountain. Forms: HEAH-
MUNTUM, *dat. pl.*

HEAHNES (OE) height, sublimity. Forms: HEAHNESSE,
dat. sing.

HEAHSÆ (OE) deep sea.

HEAHSETL (OE) high seat, throne. Forms:—, *ac. sing.*;
HEAHSETLE, *dat. sing.*; HEAHSETLUM, *dat. pl.*

HEAHÞUNOR (OE) lofty thunder. Forms: HEAHÞUNRES,
gen. sing.

HEALDAN (OE) to contain, hold, restrain. Forms:
HEALDAÞ, 3 *pres. sing.*

HEALS (OE) neck. Forms: HEALSE, *dat. sing.*

HEARD (OE) hard, harsh. Forms:—, *masc. nom. sing.*;
HEARDE, *masc. ac. pl.*

HEDLONG (Obs.) headlong, precipitous.

HEED (ME) head.

HEER (ME) here.

HEFIĠ (OE) heavy. Forms: HEFIĠU, *fem. dat. sing.*;
HEFĠUM, *masc. dat. sing.*

HEHST (OE) highest. Forms: HEHSTA, *masc. nom. sing.*

HELLE (ME) hell.

HELLEĠEAT (OE) hell's gate.

HELLSCRÆF (OE) hell's cave. Forms: HELLSCRÆFE, *dat.
sing.*

HELPEN (ME) to be of use, help. Forms: HELPEÞ, 3 *pres.
sing.*

HEM (ME) them.

HEMSELF (ME) themselves.

HEM-WARD (ME) toward them.

HENNES (ME) hence.

HENTEN (ME) to grasp, hold. Forms: HENTE, *3 p. sing.*

HEOFON (OE) heaven, sky. Forms: HEOFNES, *gen. sing.*;
        HEOFONA, *gen. pl.*

HEOFONWARE (OE) dwellers in heaven. Forms:—, *ac. pl.*

HEORTE (OE) heart. Forms: HEORTAN, *ac. pl.*

HER (OE) here.

HER (ME) to hear. Forms: HERETH, *3 pres. sing.*

HER (ME) their.

HERBE (ME) herb, plant. Forms: HERBES, *pl.*

HERCULES (L) mythic strongman and demigod, known
        for his heroic feats.

HERYHE (ME) to celebrate, glorify, praise. Forms:—, *3
        pres. sing.*

HERMUS (L) river in Asia Minor.

HERTE (ME) heart.

HERYS (ME) hairs, *pl.*

HESPER (Obs.) see HESPERUS.

HESPERUS (L) the evening star, Venus.

HEST (Obs.) behest.

HEUE (ME) to heave, lift. Forms: HEUEÞ, *3 pres. sing.*

HEUED (ME) head.

HEUEN (ME) heaven, sky. Forms: HEUENES, *pl.*

HEUIE (ME) to make heavy. Forms: HEUIEÞ, *3 pres. pl.*

HEUY (ME) heavy.

HEWE (ME) appearance. Forms: HEWES, *pl.*

HEYE (ME) high.

HEYER (ME) higher.

HEYHT(E) (ME) height, summit.

HIDER (OE, ME) hither.

HI(E) (OE) her (ac.), they.

HIERA (OE) their.

HIGHT (Obs.) called, named.

HIR (ME) their.

HIRE (OE) her (gen.)

HIR(E) (ME) her.

HIT (OE, Obs.) it.

HIW (OE) appearance, form.

HLAFORD (OE) lord. Forms: HLAFORDAS, ac. pl.

HLUT(T)OR (OE) clear, limpid. Forms:—, masc. nom. sing.;
    HLUTTRAN, masc. ac. sing.; HLUTRE, neut. dat.
    sing.

HNESĊE (OE) tender. Forms:—, masc. nom. pl.

HOISS (Obs.) to hoist. Forms: HOISSING, pres. pt.

HOLDEN (ME) to hold. Forms: HALT, 3 pres. sing.;
    HOLDEN, p. pt.

HOMER, ancient Greek epic poet, traditional author of
    the Iliad and the Odyssey.

HOND (ME) hand.

HONY (ME) honey. Forms: HONIES, pl.

HOOLY (ME) holy, sacred.

HOORE (ME) hoar.

HOOT (ME) hot.

HORNE (ME) horn. Forms: HORNES, pl.

HORS (OE, ME, Obs.) hors. Forms:—, pl. (ME).

HOUS (ME) house.

HRÆD (OE) swift. Forms: HRÆDE, *masc. ac. pl.*

HRÆDWÆĠN (OE) swift chariot. Forms: HRÆDWÆĠNE, *dat. sing.*

HRÆÞ (OE) swift. Forms: HRÆÞUM, *masc. dat. sing.;* HRÆÞE, *neut. nom. sing.*

HRERAN (OE) to excite, move. Forms: HRERENNE, *infl. inf.*

HROF (OE) roof, summit. Forms: HROFAS, *ac. pl.*

HRYRE (OE) destruction, downfall. Forms: HRYRAS, *ac. pl.;* HRYRUM, *dat. pl.*

HU (OE) how.

HUMAIN KIND (Obs.) humankind.

HUNDREÞ (ME) hundred.

HUNTE (ME) to hunt.

HURTLEN (ME) to attack, rush at. Forms: HURTLIÞ, *3 pers. sing.*

HURU (OE) indeed.

HWA (OE) what, who. Forms: HWÆT, *neut. nom. & ac.*

HWÆR (OE) where.

HWÆT (OE) ah!, lo!, what!

HWÆT (OE) brisk, vigorous. Forms: HWÆTE, *neut nom. sing.*

HWÆÞRE (OE) however, yet.

HWELĊ (OE) any, what, which.

HWEORFAN (OE) to direct, turn. Forms: HWIERFÞ, *3 pres. sing.*

HWIDER (OE) whither.

HWIERFAN (OE) to change, turn.

HWIL (OE) space of time. Phrases: ÞA HWILE, mean-
      while.

HWILUM (OE) formerly, once.

HWISPRIAN (OE) to murmur. Forms: HWISPREÞ, 3 pres.
      sing.

HWIT (OE) white. Forms: HWITAN, masc. ac. sing.

HWY (OE) why.

HYDAN (OE) to hide. Forms: HYDAÞ, pres. pl.; HYDDE, 3
      p. sing.; ĠEHYDD, p. pt.

HYDE (ME) to hide. Forms: YHID, p. pt.

HYDELS (OE) hiding place. Forms:—, pl.

HYDRA (L) nine-headed water monster, killed by Her-
      cules.

HYHE (ME) high.

HYM (ME) him, it.

HYNDE (ME) hind.

HYS (ME) his.

IĊ (OE) I.   I

IDEL (OE) idle, useless. Forms: IDLU, neut. ac. pl.

IERRE (OE) anger. Forms: IERRU, ac. pl.

ILCA (OE) same. Forms: ILCAN, nom. pl.

ILE (ME) isle.

IMPRENT (Obs.) imprint.

INDISĊ (OE) Indian. Forms: INDISĊE, neut. nom. sing.

INDUS (L) the great western river of the Indian subcon-
      tinent.

INFYNYT (ME) infinite.

INGRAUEN (Obs.) engraved, imprinted.

INHABYTAUNT (Obs.) inhabiting, resident.

INHIELDE (ME) to pour in. Forms:—, *pres. sing. subj.*

INJOYAR (Obs.) enjoyer. Forms: INJOYARS, *pl.*

INJUST (Obs.) unjust.

INNANWEARD (OE) within.

INNE (OE) inside, within.

IOYE (ME) joy.

IOYGNEN (ME) to join. Forms: JOYNETH, *3 pres. sing.*;
     IOYGNED, *p. pt.*

ITAKUS (ME) the "Ithacan," i.e., Odysseus/Ulysses.

IUGE (ME) judge.

IXION (L) Thessalian king, bound eternally to a wheel
     for attempting to rape Hera/Juno.

J   JANGLAND (ME) chattering.

JOYNEN (ME) to join. Forms: JOYNED, *3 p. sing.*

JUGE (ME) judge.

K   KEENDE (ME) nature, species.

KEMBE (ME) to adorn, comb. Forms: KEMBD, *p. pt.*

KNOWE(N) (ME) to know. Forms: KNOWE(þ)(TH), *3 pres.*
     sing.; KNOWEN, *p. pt.*

KNOWYNG (ME) knowledge.

KNYHT (ME) champion, knight, soldier.

KNYTTE (ME) to bind, unite. Forms: KNYTTEST, *2 pres.*
     sing.; KNYTTETH, *3 pres. sing.*

KRAGGE (ME) crag. Forms: KRAGGES, *pl.*

KYNG (ME) king. Forms: KYNGES, *pl.*

L   LA (OE) ah!, oh!

LÆDAN (OE) to guide, lead. Forms: LÆDENNE, *infl. inf.*;
     LÆTST, *2 pres. sing.*

LANGIAN (OE) to desire, long for.

LANGSUM (ME) lasting, prolonged.

LAÞMOD (OE) hostile.

LARGELY (ME) abundantly, generously.

LAUEN (ME) to draw, scoop. Forms: LAUED, *p. pt.*

LAWE (ME) law. Forms: LAWES, *pl.*

LEAF (OE) book leaf. Forms: LEAFE, *dat. sing.*

LECHERYE (ME) lechery, lust.

LEDEN (ME) to lead. Forms: LEDEÞ, *3 pres. sing.*

LEMES (ME) flames, *pl.*

LEMYNG (ME) shining.

LENCTEN (OE) spring. Forms: LENCTNE, *dat. sing.*

LENGHE (Obs.) length.

LERE (ME) to teach. Forms:—, *pres. sing. subj.*

LESEN (ME) to lose. Forms: LESIÞ, *3 pres. sing.*

LETTEN (ME) to delay, hinder. Forms: LETTEÞ, *3 pres. sing.*

LETTRE (ME) letter of the alphabet. Forms: LETTRES, *pl.*

LEVE (ME) to lift up. Forms: LEVED, *p. pt.*

LICGAN (OE) to lie. Forms: LIÞ, *3 pres. sing.*

LIFTE (ME) to lift. Forms: LIFTEÞ, *3 pres. sing.*

LIM (OE) limb. Forms: LIME, *dat. sing.*

L(I)(Y)OUN (ME) lion. Forms: LIOUNS, *pl.*

LITEL (ME) little.

LONGE (ME) vast.

LOOKE (ME) to consider, look at. Forms:—, *pres. sing. subj.*

LOOKE (Obs.) countenance, look.

LOOTHLY (ME) hateful, loathsome.

LORDE (ME) lord.

LOUE (ME) love.

LOUS (ME) loose, free.

LOUSE (Obs.) to loose. Forms: LOUSED, *p. pt.*

LOW(E)(H) (ME) low.

LUCIFER (L) the morning star, Venus.

LUFIAN (OE) to love. Forms: LUFA, *imp. sing.*

LUFU (OE) love. Forms: LUFE, *dat. sing.*

LUSTEN (ME) to please. Forms: LUST, *3 pres. sing.*

LUSTRE (Obs.) to lustrate, purify.

LUXURIE (ME) lust.

LYEN (ME) to lie. Forms: LIEÞ, *3 pres. sing.*

LYF (ME) life.

LYFT (OE) sky.

LYGHT (ME) light.

LYKEN (ME) to please. Forms: LYKEÞ, *3 pres. sing.*

LYM (ME) limb. Forms: LYMES, *pl.*

LYMM (Obs.) limb. Forms: LYMMS, *pl.*

LYST (ME) to please.

M MACIAN (OE) to make. Forms: MACA, *imp. sing.*

MÆĠ (OE) to be able, can. Forms: MÆĠE, *pres. sing. subj.*;
MIHTE, *3 p. sing.*

MÆĠEN (OE) strength.

MÆĠESTER (OE) master.

MÆST (OE) acorns, beachmast. Forms: MÆSTE, *dat. sing.*

MAISTER (ME) master. Forms: MAISTRES, *gen. sing.*

MAISTRIE (ME) mastery.

MAKEN (ME) to make. Forms: MAKEÞ, *3 pres. sing.*

MAKERE (ME) author, maker.

MANASE (ME) to menace. Forms: MANASSYNGE, *pres. pt.*

MANERE (ME) custom, way. Forms: MANERES, *pl.*

MANNCYNN (OE) mankind.

M(A)(O)NN (OE) man, person. Forms: MENN, *nom. pl.*;
    MONNA, *gen. pl.*

MARGARIT (ME) pearl. Forms: MARGARITS, *pl.*

MARMORYK (ME) from Marmorica, a region in Roman
    North Africa.

MARYNER (ME) mariner, sailor. Forms: MARYNERS, *pl.*

MATER (ME) material, matter.

MAÞM (OE) treasure. Forms: MAÞMAS , *ac. pl.*

MAWE (ME) liver, stomach.

MEARC (OE) boundary, limit. Forms: MEARCE, *ac. sing.*;
    MEARCAS, *ac. pl.*; MEARCUM, *dat. pl.*

MEDE (Obs.) meed, reward.

MEDLE (ME) to mix, muddle. Forms: MEDLEÞ, MEDLYÞ,
    3 pres. sing.; MED(E)LYNG, *pres. pt.*

MELLE (ME) to mingle, mix.

MENĠAN (OE) to mix. Forms: ĠEMENĠED, *p. pt.*

MERVEILLOUS (ME) miraculous.

MESTIER (ME) function, occupation. Forms: MESTIERS, *pl.*

MESURE (ME) moderation, proportion.

METE (ME) fitting, meet.

METE (ME) food, meal. Forms: METES, *pl.*

MID (OE) with.

MIERCE (OE) dark, murky. Forms:—, *masc. ac. pl.*;
    MIERCUM, *neut. dat. pl.*

MILDSIAN (OE) to be mercicul. Forms: MILDSA, *imp. sing.*

MISLIĊ (OE) diverse, various. Forms: MISLICUM, *dat. pl.*

MISWENDAN (OE) to misdirect, pervert. Forms: MISWENT, *3 pres. sing.*

MIÞAN (OE) to conceal, hide. Forms: MIÞÞ, *3 pres. sing.*

MIXT (Obs.) mingled, mixed.

MOCHEL (ME) much.

MOCYOUN (ME) motion, movement. Forms: MO-CYOUNS, *pl.*

MOD (OE) mind. Forms: MODES, *gen. sing.*; MODE, *dat. sing.*

MODER (ME) mother. Forms: MODER, MODRES, *gen. sing.*

MODĠEÞOHT (OE) mind, thought.

MOEUE(N) (ME) to move. Forms: MEVEÞ, MOEUEÞ, *3 pres. sing.*; MOEUYNG, *pres. pt.*; IMOEUID, *p. pt.*

MO(E)UYNG(E) (ME) motion, movement. Forms: MOEUYNGES, *pl.*

MON (OE) one, person.

MONSTAR (Obs.) monster. Forms: MONSTARS, *pl.*

MONTAYGNE (ME) mountain. Forms: MONTAYGNES, *pl.*

MO(O)NE (ME) moon.

MO(O)T (ME) may, must (*v.*). Forms:—, *3 pres. sing.*, *pres. subj. sing.*

MORÞRE (ME) to murder. Forms: YMORÞRED, *p. pt.*

MOT (OE) may, (*v.*).

MOUNTE (ME) to mount.

MOUÞE (ME) mouth. Forms: MOUÞES, *pl.*

MOWEN (ME) to be able. Forms: MAIST, *2 pres. sing.*; MYHTEN, *3 pres. pl.*

MUNT (OE) mountain. Forms: MUNTES, *gen. sing.*

MYGHT (ME) might, power.

MYGHTY (ME) mighty.

MYND (Obs.) mind. Forms: MYNDZ, *gen. sing.*; *pl.*

MYRIE (ME) pleasant.

MYS-WEY (ME) byway. Forms: MIS-WEYES, *pl.*

NÆFÞ (OE) have not=NE HÆFÞ, *3 pres. sing.*

NÆFRE (OE) never.

NÆNIĠ (OE) none=NE + ÆNIĠ. Forms: NÆNIĠU, *neut.*
    ac. pl.

NÆS (OE) was not=NE WÆS.

NAN (OE) no, none.

NANÞING (OE) nothing. Forms:—, *ac. sing.*

NANWIHT (OE) nothing. Forms: NANWIHTE, *dat. sing.*

NARWE (ME) narrow.

NAT (ME) not.

NAÞEL(A)(E)S (ME) nevertheless.

NAUHT (OE) naught, nothing.

NAWIHT (OE) naught, nothing. Forms: NAWIHTES, *gen.*
    sing.

NE (OE, ME) not. Phrases: NE...NE, neither...nor.

NEARRA (OE) nearer.

NEARWIAN (OE) to become compressed, narrow. Forms:
    NEARWAÞ, *3 pres. sing.*

NEKKE (ME) neck. Forms: NEKKES, *pl.*

NEMEAN, of Nemea in ancient Greece; the wild Nemean
    lion was killed and flayed by Hercules.

NERO (L) Nero Claudius Caesar (37-68 A.D.), emperor
    of Rome. 54-68 A.D.

NETT (OE) net.

NEYE (ME) nigh.

NIHT (OE) night.

NIHTGLOM (OE) darkness of night. Forms: NIHT-GLOMES, *gen. sing.*

NIMAN (OE) to take. Forms: NIMÞ, *3 pres. sing.*

NIS (OE, ME) is not=NE IS.

NIÞER (OE) downward.

NIÞERWEARD(ES) (OE) downward.

NIÞOR (OE) lower.

NIÞRE (OE) below.

NOGHT-FOR-THAT (ME) nevertheless.

NOLDE (OE, ME) will not=NE WOLDE.

NON (ME) none.

NOON (ME) no (preceding a vowel or *h*).

NOOT (ME) knows not=NE + WOOT.

NORISSE (ME) to nourish. Forms: NORYSHED, *p. pt.*

NOTUS (L) the south wind.

NOUMBRE (ME) astronomy, number.

NOUÞER (ME) neither.

NOYOUS (ME) troublesome.

NU (OE) now.

NY (Obs.) nigh.

NYLL (ME) not to will, not to wish=NE WYL. Forms:—, *3 pres. sing.*

NYLLAN (OE) not to will, not to wish=NE WILLAN. Forms: NYLLE, *3 pres. sing.*

O   OCCIAN (ME) ocean.

OF (OE) from.

OFDÆL (OE) down-sloping.

OFDUNE (OE) downward.

OFEN (OE) furnace, oven. Forms: OFNUM, *dat. pl.*

OFERCUMAN (OE) to overcome, subdue.

OFEREORÞFÆST (OE) too earthbound.

OFERSEON (OE) to despise, survey. Forms: OFER-
SEONNE, *infl. inf.*; OFERSIEHÞ, *3 pres. sing.*

OFERTREDAN (OE) to trample upon. Forms: OFER-
TREDAÞ, *3 pres. pl.*

OFERWINNAN (OE) to defeat. Forms: OFERWANN, *3 p.
sing.*

OFFLEOGAN (OE) to fly away. Forms: OFFLEOGE, *pres.
sing. subj.*

OFSHOWVE (ME) to shove away.

OFSLAY (Obs.) to slay. Forms: OFSLEN, *p. pt.*

OGHT (ME) anything.

O(O)LDE (ME) former, old.

ONDRÆDAN (OE) to fear. Forms: ONDRÆDAÞ, *3 pres.
pl.*; ONDRÆDE, *pres. subj. sing.*

ONĠEAN-FLOWENDE (OE) flowing back.

ONĠIETAN (OE) to know, perceive. Forms: ONĠIETT, *3
pres. sing.*; ONĠIETAÞ, *1 pres. pl.*

ONLÆTAN (OE) to loosen.

ONLIHTAN (OE) to enlighten, illuminate. Forms:
ONLIHTAÞ, *3 pres. sing.*

ONLOFTE (ME) on high.

ON-LONG (ME) along.

ONSĊUNIAN (OE) to reject, shun. Forms: ONSĊUNAÞ,
    3 pres. sing.

ONSEON (OE) to look at. Forms: ONSEAH, *3 p. sing.*

ONSTYRIAN (OE) to agitate the mind, disturb. Forms:
    ONSTYRIAÞ, *3 pres. pl.*

ONWÆFLIAN (OE) to cause to talk foolishly. Forms:
    ONWÆFLIĠE, *pres. sing. subj.*

OO (ME) one.

OPPREST (Obs.) oppressed.

OPPRISSING (Obs.) suppressing.

ORDENA(U)NCE (ME) arrangement, order.

ORDRE (ME) order.

ORPHEUS (L) mythical Thracian bard, son of Calliope
    the muse of poetry, and husband of Eurydice.

ORWIERÞU (OE) dishonor, shame. Forms: ORWIERÞE,
    ac. sing.

OÞER (OE, ME) other. Forms: OÞERE, *pl.* (ME)

OÞFLEON (OE) to flee. Forms: OÞFLIEHÞ, *3 pres. sing.*

OÞÞE (OE) or.

OUER (ME) above, on, over; too, very.

OUERCUMAN (ME) to overcome. Forms: OUERCUMEN,
    p. pt.

OUERT (ME) open.

OUERÞROW(I)YNG(E) (ME) headlong, overwhelming,
    precipitous, rotating.

OUTLAWID (ME) outlawed.

OW(E)NE (ME) own.

OWT (ME) out.

P PACEFIE (Obs.) to pacify, soothe.

PALE (ME) to make pale. Forms: PALEÞ, *3 pres. sing.*

PANCHE (Obs.) paunch.

PARTIE (ME) part. Forms: PARTIES, *pl.*

PARTZ (Obs.) parts, *(pl.)*

PAS (Obs.) to step.

PAYS (ME) heaviness.

PAÞE (ME) path.

PEES (ME) peace.

PERCEN (ME) to pierce.

PERFIT (ME) perfect.

PERTEYNE (ME) to pertain. Forms: PERTEYNETH, *3 pres. sing.*

PESE (ME) to appease. Forms: PESID, *3 p. sing.*

PEYNE (ME) pain, punishment.

PHOEBUS (L) the sun.

PHOLIFEMUS (L) the one-eyed giant Polyphemus.

PHRYGIA (L) region of Asia Minor where the ancient city of Troy was located.

PLAIN (Obs.) to complain about. Forms: PLAINING, *pres. pt.*

PLANETE (ME) planet. Forms: PLANETES, *gen. sing.*

PLAYNYNG (Obs) complaining.

PLEASAUNT (ME) pleasant, pleasing.

PLEIYING (ME) playful.

PLENTEE (ME) plenty.

PLEYEN (ME) to play, sport. Forms: PLEYEÞ, *3 pres. sing.*

PLOUNGEN (ME) to bathe, plunge. Forms: YPLOUNGED, *p. pt.*

PLOUNGY (ME) rainy, stormy.

POCIOUN (ME) potion. Forms: POCIOUNS, *pl.*

POUPPE (ME) ship's stern. Forms: POUPPES, *pl.*

POWRE (Obs.) power, strength.

POYNTEL (ME) stylus.

PRAVE (Obs.) depraved, perverse.

PREOST (OE) priest.

PRESSEN (ME) to press, weigh down. Forms: PRESSID,
      p. pt.

PREST (Obs.) pressed, weighed down.

PREUEN (ME) to prove. Forms: PREUEÞ, *3 pres. sing.*

PRIKKE (ME) goad, pricking. Forms: PRIKKES, *pl.*

PRIUE (ME) secret.

PROUDE (ME, Obs.) proud.

PROPRE (ME) own, peculiar.

PURP(U)R(E) (ME) purple.

Q QUAKE (ME) to tremble. Forms: QUAKITH, *3 pres. sing.*

QUIKE (ME) alive, living.

R RAINE (Obs.) rein. Forms: RAINES, *pl.*

RAMPAR (Obs.) rampart.

RAÞER (ME) earlier, former.

RAÞEST (ME) earliest, first.

RAUYSSYNG (ME) seizing.

RAVEYN (ME) greed, rapaciousness.

RAVYNOUS (ME) greedy, hungry.

RAYNE (Obs.) rein. Forms: RAYNES, *pl.*

RAYSE (Obs.) to raise, rouse up. Forms: RAYSES, *3 pres.*
      sing.

REĊĊERE (OE) ruler.

RECCHEN (ME) to care, care about. Forms: RECCHEÞ, 3
     pres. sing.

RECLAIM (Obs.) to call back.

RECLEYME (ME) to call back, recall. Forms: RECLEYMING,
     pres. pt.

RECOURSE (ME) course. Forms: RECOURSES, *pl.*

REDDIS SEA (Obs.) Red Sea.

REDE (ME) red.

REDY (ME) red, ruddy.

REFOWSESTOW (ME) you refuse=REFUSEST ÞOU.

REFUSEN (ME) to refuse. Forms: REFUSEST, 3 *pres. sing.*

REFUT (ME) refuge.

REĠEN (OE) rain.

REGNEN (ME) to reign.

REIOISEN (ME) to rejoice. Forms:—, *pres. pl.*

REMEMBREN (ME) to remember. Forms: REMEMBRIÞ, 3
     pres. sing.

RENNE (ME) to run. Forms:—, *pres. subj. sing.*

RENNYNG (ME) running.

REPEYRE (ME) to return. Forms: REPEYREÞ, 3 *pres. pl.*;
     REPEYRING, *p. pt.*

REPREVE (ME) to reproach. Forms: REPREUIÞ, 3 *pres. sing.*

RESOLUE (Obs.) to melt. Forms: RESOLUES, 3 *pres. sing.*

RESOUN (ME) reason.

RESOUNE (ME) to resound. Forms: RESOUNYNG, *pres. pt.*

RESTRAIN (Obs.) restraint.

RESTREYNE (ME) to hold in check. Forms:—, *pres. sing.
     subj.*

RETOURNE (ME) to return. Forms: RETOURNETH, *3 pres. sing.*

RETOURS (Obs.) return.

REWLEN (ME) to control, govern, rule. Forms: REWLEST, *2 pres. sing.*; REWLEÞ, *3 pres. sing.*; ROULIDE, *3 p. sing.*; REWLING, *pres. pt.*

REYNE (Obs.) to rein.

RICHESSE (ME) riches, wealth.

RIHT (OE) just.

RIHTRYNE (OE) proper course. Forms: RIHTRYNAS, *ac. pl.*

RIGHTWISA (OE) the righteous. Forms: RIHTWISUM, *dat. pl.*

RIHTWISE (ME) the righteous.

RI(Y)UER(E) (ME) river.

ROMEBURG (OE) Rome.

ROMEN (ME) to roam. Forms: ROMEÞ, *3 pres. sing.*

ROO (ME) roe deer. Forms: ROOS, *pl.*

ROSEN(E) (ME) rose-colored.

ROUNDE (ME) circle, orbit. Forms: ROUNDES, *pl.*

RYHT (ME)(right reason. Forms: RYHTES, *pl.*

RYHTFUL (ME) just, rightful.

RYNE (OE) course, orbit. Forms:——, *ac. sing.*; RYNAS, *ac. pl.*

S SÆD (OE) seed. Forms: SÆDE, *dat. sing.*

SANDZ (Obs.) sands, *pl.*

SANZ (ME) without.

SAR (OE) pain, sorrow.

SAUF (ME) safe.

SAUOR (Obs.) savor. Forms: SAVORS, *pl.*

SAWAN (OE) to sow. Forms: SÆWEST, 2 *pres. sing.*

SAWOL (OE) soul. Forms: SAWLA, *ac. pl.*

SAYL (ME) sails. Forms: SAYLES, *pl.*

SĊEADUHELM (OE) darkness. Forms: SĊEADUHELME, *dat. sing.*

SĊEARD (OE) deprived of.

SĊEARPNES (OE) perception, sharpness of mind. Forms: SĊEARPNESSE, *gen. sing.*

SCHE (ME) she.

SCHYRE (ME) bright, clear.

SĊIEPPEND (OE) creator.

SĊINAN (OE) to shine. Forms: SĊINAÞ, 3 *pres. sing.*

SCIPP (ME) ship. Forms: SCIPPS, *pl.*

SĊIR (OE) sheer, white. Forms: SĊIRE, *ac. pl.*

SĊIROR (OE) more brightly.

SCOM (ME) froth, lather. Forms: SCOMES, *pl.*

SCORKLE (ME) to scorch. Forms: SCORKLITH, 3 *pres. sing.*

SĊULDOR (OE) shoulder. Forms: SĊULDRU, *ac. pl.*

SE (OE) the.

SEAKE (Obs.) to seek.

SEAR (OE) dry, sere. Forms: SEARRE, *fem. dat. sing.*

SEĊAN (OE) to seek. Forms: SECST, 2 *pres. sing.*; SECÞ, 3 *pres. sing.*

SECRE (ME) private, secret.

SEE (ME) sea.

SEEN (ME) to see. Forms: SEEST, 2 *pres. sing.*; SEOÞ, 3 *pres. sing*; YSEIN, *p. pt.*

SEKE (ME) to seek. Forms: SEKEÞ, SEKITH, 3 *pres. sing.*; SEKEN, *pres. pl.*

SEKESTOW (ME) you seek=SEKEST ÞOU.

SELD (ME) seldom.

SELF (OE) self. Forms: SELFRE, *dat. sing.*

SELFWILLES (OE) voluntarily.

SELUESAME (Obs.) selfsame.

SEMBLABLE (ME) similar.

SEME (ME) to appear, seem. Forms: SEMEÞ, 3 *pres. sing.*

SENCE (Obs.) sense. Forms: SENCIS, *pl.*

SENYTH (ME) zenith.

SEON (OE) to see. Forms: SIHST, 2 *pres. sing.*; SIEHÞ, 3 *pres. sing.*; SEAH, 3 *p. sing.*

SENATOUR (ME) elder, senator. Forms: SENATOURS, *pl.*

SEPTEMTRIONES (L) the seven stars of the northern constellation Ursa Major.

SERCHE (Obs.) to search.

SESOUN (ME) season. Forms: SESOUNS, *pl.*

SETL (OE) seat.

SETTAN (OE) to establish, set. Forms: SETT, *p. pt.*

SETTE (ME) to set.

SHADWE (ME) shadow. Forms: SHADWES, *pl.*

SHAL (ME, Obs.) shall. Forms: SHOLDE, 3 *p. sing.*

SHEDE (ME) to scatter, shed. Forms: SHAD, YSHED, *p. pt.*

SHELVING (Obs.) sloping. Forms: SHELVINGS, *pl.*

SHEWE (ME) to show.

SHILD (Obs.) shield.

SHIPP (ME) ship. Forms: SHIPPES, *pl.*

SHREWE (ME) bad person, wretch.

SHYNE(N) (ME) to shine. Forms: SHYNE, *imp. sing.*

SIBB (OE) peace, relationship. Forms: SIBBE, *ac. sing.*

SIKER (ME) secure, sure.

SINGAL (OE) continuous. Forms:—, *neut. ac. sing.*;
   SINGALE, *fem. ac. sing.*

S(I)(Y)NGULER (ME) separate, single.

SINT see BEON.

SIRIUS (L) the Dog Star, brightest in the sky.

SITHE (Obs.) to seethe. Forms: SITHING, *pres. pt.*

SITTAN (OE) to sit. Forms: SIT(T), *3 pres. sing.*; SITTE,
   pres. sing. subj.

SITTEN (ME) to sit. Forms: SITTEN, *3 pres. pl.*

SKANT (ME) scant.

SKATTERD (Obs.) scattered.

SLÆC (OE) slow, tardy. Forms:—, *masc. nom. sing.*

SLÆP (OE) sleep.

SLAKED (Obs.) loosed.

SLIDYNG (ME) flowing, *pres. pt.*

SLIPPAR (Obs.) fleeting, unstable.

SMÆCC (OE) taste.

SMAL (ME) minor part, small thing.

SMARAGDE (ME) emerald. Forms: SMARAGDES, *pl.*

SMYLTE (OE) serene. Forms: SMYLTUM, *neut. dat. sing.*

SODENLY (ME) suddenly.

SOFTE (ME) gentle, soft.

SOKING (Obs.) absorbent.

SOL (L, OE, Obs.) sun.

SOLEYNE (ME) alone, sole.

SOMETYME (ME) once, at a certain time.

SOM (ME) some.

SOMME (ME) totality, whole.

SOMOCHE (Obs.) so much.

SONCRÆFT (OE) music.

SONGE (ME) song. Forms: SONGES, SONGEZ, *pl.*

SONNE (ME) sun.

SOONE (ME) at once, soon.

SO(O)TH (ME) truth.

SOR (ME) sorrowful, sorry.

SORGFULL (OE) sorrowfull.

SORGLEOÞ (OE) dirge, sorrow-song. Forms:—, *pl.*

SORWE (ME) grief, sorrow.

SORWYNG(E) (ME) sorrowing. Forms: SORWYNGES, *pl.*

SOÞ (OE) truly.

SOÞELY (ME) truly.

SOÞENESSE (ME) truth.

SOÞNES (OE) truth. Forms: SOÞNESSUM, *dat. pl.*

SOUERYN(E) (ME) highest, supreme.

SOULE (ME) soul. Forms: SOULES, *gen. pl.*

SOUNEN (ME) to sound, resound. Forms: SOUNE, *pres. subj. sing.*

SOUNYNG (ME) roaring, sounding.

SOWSE (Obs.) to plunge, souse.

SPERE (ME) sphere. Forms: SPERES, *pl.*

SPOR (OE) spoor, track, trail.

SPREDEN (ME) to spread. Forms: Y-SPRADDE, *p. pt.*

SPRINGAN (OE) to spring. Forms: SPRINGAÞ, *3 pres. pl.*

STÆPE (OE) step.

STÆPPAN (OE) to step. Forms: STÆPPE, *1 pres. sing.*

STANDAN (OE) to stand. Forms: STENT, *3 pres. sing.*;
     STANDAÞ, *3 pres. pl.*

STARIAN (OE) to stare. Forms: STARAÞ, *3 pres. sing.*

STAÞOLFÆST (OE) firm, stabile. Forms: STAÞOLFÆSTE,
     fem. ac. sing. & pl.

STEARC (OE) rough, violent. Forms: STEARCE, *masc. ac. pl.*

STEDFAST (ME) steadfast.

STEORRA (OE) star.

STERRY (ME) starry.

STIĊE (OE) prick, stab. Forms:—, *dat. sing.*

STIERN (ME) stern.

STILLE (ME) quiet.

STINGAN (OE) to pierce, stab, sting. Forms: STINGÞ, *3
     pres. sing.*

STIORAN (OE) to steer. Forms: STIOREÞ, *3 pres. sing.*

STOA (L) from the Greek, referring to the long "Portico"
     in ancient Athens where the Stoic philosophers
     taught.

STOKKES (ME) tree trunks, *pl.*

STONDEN (ME) to stand up, stop.

STOON (ME) stone.

STORM (OE) storm. Forms: STORMAS, *ac. pl.*

STRAICT (Obs.) straightway.

STRAITEN (Obs.) to confine, make narrow.

STRAKE (Obs.) stretched out, *3. p. sing.*

STRAND (OE) shore. Forms: STRANDE, *dat. sing.*;
     STRAND, *ac. pl.*

STRAUGHT (ME) stretched.

STRAUNGER (ME) stranger.

STREAM (OE) river, running water. Forms: STREAMAS, *nom. pl.*

STREEM (ME) river, stream. Forms: STREMES, *pl.*

STRE(I)(Y)TE (ME) narrow.

STRENG (ME) string. Forms: STRENGES, *pl.*

STRENGH (Obs.) strength.

STRENGÞE (ME) force, strength. Forms: STRENGÞES, *pl.*

STRENÞU (OE) strength.

STREPE (ME) to strip. Forms:—, *pres. subj. sing.*

STRONGE HOLD (Obs.) stronghold.

STUDIE (ME) zeal, devotion, study.

STYĊĊE (OE) piece. Forms: STYĊĊUM, *dat. pl.*

STYMPHALIAN (L) of Lake Stymphalus in ancient Greece; the man-eating flock of Stymphalian birds was destroyed by Hercules.

STYRRE (Obs.) to stir. Forms: STYRRING, *pres. pt.*

SUBGIT (ME) subject (*adj.*).

SUCHE (Obs.) such.

SUFFERANTLY (Obs.) submissively.

SUFFAR (Obs.) to suffer. Forms: SUFFARS, *3 pres. sing.*

SUFFRE (ME) to allow, endure. Forms: SUFFRIÞ, *3 pres. sing.*

SUITE (Obs.) suit.

SUMORHÆTE (OE) summer's heat.

SUNDRE (ME) to divide, separate. Forms: I-SUNDRED, *p. pt.*

SUNNE (OE) sun. Forms: SUNNAN, *gen. sing.*

SURMOUNTEN (ME) to surmount, surpass. Forms:
SURMOUNTEÞ, *3 pres. sing.*

SWA (OE) so, as.

SWAPAN (OE) to seep. Forms: SWAPAÞ, *3 pres. pl.*

SWEART (OE) black. Forms:—, *masc. nom. sing.*

SWELĊE (OE) such. Forms: SWELĊE, *fem. ac. sing.*

SWELTRY (Obs.) sultry, sweltering.

SWETE (ME) sweet, precious.

SWEORD (OE) sword.

SWEYE (ME) sway, whirl.

SWICH(E) (ME) such.

SWIFT (OE) swift. Forms: SWIFTE, *fem. ac. pl.*

SW(I)(Y)FTE (ME) swift.

SWIFTIST (Obs.) swiftist.

SWILKE (ME) such.

SWINGAN (OE) to afflict, beat, strike. Forms: SWINGÞ, *3 pres. sing.*

SWITEST (Obs.) sweetest.

SWYNE (ME) swine. Forms:—, *pl.*

SWOLOWE (ME) to swallow. Forms: SWOLWYNG, *pres. pt.*

SWOLN (Obs.) swollen.

SWUTOL (OE) evident, manifest. Forms: SWUTOLU, *neut. nom. pl.*

SYN (ME) after, since.

SYNGEN (ME) to sing. Forms: SYNGETH, *3 pres. sing.*

TAGUS (L) Iberian river.   **T**

TANGELL (Obs.) to tangle. Forms:—, *3 pres. pl.*

TANTALUS (L) Lydian, or Phrygian, king condemned to
        eternal hunger and thirst.

TARIEN (ME) to delay. Forms: TARIEÞ, *3 pres. sing.*

TEER (ME) tear. Forms: TERES, *pl.*

TELLEN (ME) to consider as, count. Forms: YTALD, *p. pt.*

TERE (ME) to tear. Forms: TEREÞ, *3 pres. sing.*

ÞA (OE) the, that (*dem.*), *fem. ac. sing. & pl.*

ÞÆM (OE) the, that (*dem.*), *masc. & neut. dat. sing., dat.
        pl. (all genders).*

ÞÆR (OE) there.

ÞÆRE (OE) the, that (*dem.*), *fem. ac. sing.*

ÞÆS (OE) the, that (*dem.*), *masc. & neut. gen. sing.*

ÞÆT (OE) the, that (*dem.*), *neut. nom. sing.*

ÞÆTTE (OE) so that.

ÞAN (ME) than, then.

ÞANNE (OE) then.

ÞAT (ME) that.

ÞAÞA (OE) when.

ÞAYRE (ME) their.

ÞE (OE) that, which, who.

ÞE (ME) the.

ÞE (ME) thee.

ÞEI (ME) they.

ÞERE (ME) their.

ÞERE (ME) there.

ÞES (OE) this, *masc. nom. sing.*

ÞI (ME) thy.

ÞILKE (ME) the same.

ÞIN (OE) thine, thy.

ÞING (OE, ME) thing. Forms:—, nom. & ac. pl. (OE);
   ÞING, ÞINGES, pl. (ME); ÞINGA, gen. pl. (OE).

ÞINNE (ME) fine, thin.

ÞIS (OE) this, neut. nom. sing.

ÞIS (ME) this.

ÞISE (ME) these.

ÞO (ME) those.

THOGH (ME, Obs.) though.

THOGHT (ME) mind, thought.

ÞONE (OE) the, that (dem.), masc. ac. sing.

ÞORN (OE) thorn, thornbush. Forms: ÞORNAS, ac. pl.

ÞORNE BUSK (ME) thornbush.

THOROW (Obs.) through.

THOS (Obs.) those.

ÞOUGH (ME) though.

ÞRAL (ME) subject (adj.).

ÞREST (ME) to press, thrust down on.

THRETEN (ME) to menace, threaten. Forms: THRETYNG,
   pres. pt.

ÞRIFT (ME) profit.

ÞRI-HEAFDEDE (OE) three-headed.

ÞRIST (ME) thirst.

THRO (Obs.) through.

ÞROTE (ME) throat.

ÞRUST (ME) thirst.

THRYVE (ME) to thrive. Forms: ÞRIUEÞ, 3 pres. sing.;
   THROF, 3 p. sing.

ÞU (OE) thou.

ÞURGH (ME) through.

ÞURH (OE) through.

ÞURHFARAN (OE) to penetrate, pierce. Forms: ÞURH-
FARAÞ, *3 pres. pl.*

ÞURHFAREN (ME) to travel through. Forms: ÞURH-
FAREÞ, *3 pres. sing.*

ÞURHSEON (OE) to see through. Forms: ÞURHSIEHÞ, *3
pres. sing.*

ÞUS (OE, ME) thus.

ÞUSWISE (ME) in this manner.

ÞY LÆS (OE) lest.

TID (OE) season, time. Forms:—, *ac. sing.*

TIDE (ME) time, hour.

TIGRE (ME) tiger.

TIGRIS (L) with the Euphrates, one of the two chief riv-
ers of Mesopotamia.

TIJINGE (Obs.) tying.

TITYUS (L) giant, condemned eternally to have his liver
eaten by a vulture for attempting to rape Latona/
Leto.

TOCLEVE (ME) to split apart.

TODRAWEN (ME) to attract, pull. Forms: TODRAWE, *3
pres. sing.*

TODRIFAN (OE) to disperse, drive away. Forms: TODRIF,
imp. sing.; TODRIFEN, *p. pt.*

TO HEUENE-WARD (ME) toward heaven.

TOLIESAN (OE) to loosen, separate.

TOSHAKEN (ME) to shake to pieces. Forms: TOSHAKE,
p. pt.

TOSK (ME) tusk.

TO-TEREN (ME) to tear apart. Forms: TO-TORE, *p. pt.*

TOÞER (ME) the other = THE + OÞER.

TOUR (ME) tower. Forms: TOURES, *pl.*

TOURNE (Obs.) to turn. Forms:——, *2 pres. pl.*

TOWEARD (OE) toward. Phrases: TO...WEARD.

TRAAS (ME) trace.

TRAUILEN (ME) to labor, toil. Forms: TRAUILEÞ, *3 pres. sing.*

TRAUAYLE (ME) labor. Forms: TRAUAYLES, *pl.*

TREBILL (ME) triple.

TREDAN (OE) to tredan, trample. Forms: TREDAÞ, *3 pres. sing.*

TREOWFÆSTNES (OE) faithfulness. Forms: TREOW-FÆSTNESSE, *dat. sing.*

TREWE (ME) loyal, true.

TREWE (ME) truce. Forms: TREWES, *pl.*

TRIEWE (OE) faithful, trusty. Forms: TRIEWAN, *gen. sing.*

TROTHE (Obs.) truth. Forms: TROUTHES, *pl.*

TUNGE (OE) tongue. Forms: TUNGAN, *ac. pl.*

TURNEN (ME) to turn. Forms: TURNE, *pres. sing. subj.*

TWYES (ME) twice.

TYRAUNT (ME) tyrant. Forms: TYRAUNTES, *pl.*

TYRE (ME) Tyrian.

TYRIENE (ME) Tyrian.

TYRNAN (OE) to turn. Forms: TYRNEST, *2 pres. sing.*; TYRNEÞ, *3 pres. sing.*

TYRRHEN (Obs.) Tyrrhenian.

℧ UFAN (OE) downward, from above.

ULTIMA THULE (L) "far" Thule, mythic island in the
   north.

UNÆÞELE (OE) degenerate, ignoble.

UNBEGAN (OE) uncultivated, untilled.

UNDERBÆC (OE) back, backward.

UNDERFOTE (ME) underfoot.

UNDERLICGAN (OE) to submit. Forms: UNDERLIÞ, 3
   pres. sing.

UNDERPUT (Obs.) to subject.

UNKNOWE (ME) unknown.

UNKNOWYNG (ME) ignorant, unknowying.

UNKYNDELY (ME) cruelly, unnaturally.

UNLES (Obs.) unless.

UNMÆHTIĠ (OE) unmighty. Forms: UNMÆHTIĠES, gen.
   sing.

UNRIHT (OE) unjust. Forms: UNRIHTRE, fem. dat. sing.

UNRIHTDÆD (OE) wrongdoing. Forms: UNRIHTDÆDE,
   nom. pl.

UNSAD (ME) unstable.

UNSTILNES (OE) emotion, mental agitation. Forms:
   UNSTILNESSE, ac. sing.

UNTRIEWE (OE) unfaithful, untrue. Forms: UNTRIEWU,
   fem. nom. sing.

UNWAR (ME) unaware.

UNWIS (OE) ignorant.

UNWISNES (OE) ignorance. Forms: UNWISNESSE, gen.
   sing.

UNWIT (ME) folly, ignorance.

UNWON (Obs.) unconquered.

UPHURL (Obs.) to hurl up. Forms: UPHURLING, *pres. pt.*

UPRIGHT (OE) upright, upward.

UPRODOR (OE) sky. Forms:—, *ac. sing.*

UPSPRING (OE) birth, sunrise.

URE (OE) our.

USAN (ME) to employ, use.

UT (OE) out, outside.

UTT(E)REST (ME) furthest.

VADING (Obs.) elusive, evading. **V**

VARIENGE (ME) change. Forms: VARIENGES, *pl.*

VENGERISSE (ME) female avenger. Forms: VENGERISSES, *pl.*

VENYM (ME) poison. Forms: VENYMS, *pl.*

VERRAY (ME) real, true.

VESUVIUS (L) volcano in southwest Italy.

VEXEN (ME) to vex, worry. Forms: VEXE, *3 pres. pl.*

VEYN(E) (ME) vain.

VIL (ME) vile.

VNFOLDE (ME) to unfold.

VNSLACKED (Obs.) unslackened.

VNWEMMED (ME) untouched.

VOYS (ME) voice.

VPRYHT (ME) upright.

WÆFAN (OE) to cover, envelope. Forms: WÆFÞ, *3 pres.* **W**
sing.

WÆĠN (OE) carriage, chariot.

WÆTA (OE) moisture.

WÆTER (OE) water. Forms:—, *ac. pl.*

WÆTERĠEFEALL (OE) waterfall. Forms: WÆTER-
　　　ĠEFEALLA, *gen. pl.*

WÆTRIAN (OE) to irrigate, water. Forms: WÆTRAÞ, 3
　　　pres. sing.

WAIGHT (Obs.) weight. Forms: WAIGHTS, *pl.*

WAILE (Obs.) to wail. Forms: WAILES, 3 *pres. sing.*

WA(I)(Y)N(E) (ME) carriage, cart, chariot. Forms:
　　　WAYNES, *pl.*

WALD (ME) forest. Forms: WALDES, *pl.*

WALKEN (ME) to walk.

WALWE (ME) to roil, toss. Forms: WALWYNG, *pres. pt.*

WAMFULL (OE) defiled, impure. Forms: WAMFULLUM,
　　　fem. dat. pl.

WANDRING (Obs.) wandering. Forms: WANDRINGS, *pl.*

WANDRYNG (ME) wandering, *pres. pt.*

WANIAN (OE) to fade, wane. Forms: WANIAÞ, 3 *pres. pl.*

WASSHE(N) (ME) to steep, wash. Forms: WESSH, 3 *pres.*
　　　sing.

WATRE (ME) water. Forms: WATRES, *pl.*

WAWE (ME) wave. Forms: WAWES, *pl.*

WAYMENTEN (ME) to lament. Forms: WAYMENTING,
　　　pres. pt.

WEALD (OE) control, dominion, power. Forms: WEALDE,
　　　dat. sing.

WEALDAN (OE) to rule, wield. Forms: WELTST, 2 *pres.*
　　　sing.; WELT, 3 *pres. sing.*; WEOLD, 3 *p. sing.*

WEALDLEÞER (OE) rein. Forms: WEALDLEÞRUM, *dat.*
　　　pl.

WEARM (OE) warm. Forms: WEARMAN, *masc. dat. sing.*

WEBB (OE) tapestry, web.

WEDER (OE) weather. Forms: WEDRE, *dat. sing.*

WEDLOK (Obs.) wedlock.

WEEPLY (ME) tearful.

WEILAWEI (OE) woe alas!

WEL (OE) well (*adv.*).

WELDEN (ME) to control. Forms:—, *3 pres. pl.*

WELK(E)(Y)N (ME) heavens, sky.

WELFUL (ME) happy, prosperous.

WELLE (ME) font, wellspring. Forms: WELLES, *pl.*

WENDAN (OE) to change, redirect. Forms: WENDRE, *fem. ac. p. pt.*

WENDEN (ME) to go. Forms: WENTE, *3 p. sing.*

WENAN (OE) to hope, expect. Forms: WENE, *pres. subj. sing.*

WENGE (ME) wing. Forms: WENGES, *pl.*

WEPE(N) (ME) to weep. Forms: WEPYNG, *pres. pt.*; WEPYD, *3 p. sing.*

WEORÐAN (OE) to become. Forms: WIERÞ, *3 pres. sing.*

WERBI (ME) whereby.

WERĠIAN (OE) to exhaust. weary. Forms: WERĠAÞ, *3 pres. pl.*

WERIE (ME) to fatigue, make weary. Forms: WERIETH, *3 pres. sing.*

WERK (ME) work.

WERRE (OE, ME) war. Forms:—, *dat. sing.* (OE); WERRES, *pl.* (ME).

WESTREN (ME) western.

WEXE (ME) to grow. Forms: WEXEN, *pres. pl.*; YWOXEN,
      p. pt.

WEY (ME) manner, means, path, way.

WHAN (ME, Obs.) when.

WHELE (ME) wheel.

WHELWE (ME) to roll, toss. Forms: WHELWEÞ, *3 pres.*
      sing.

WHENNES (ME) whence.

WHERTO (ME) why.

WHICHE (ME) which.

WHIE (Obs.) why.

WHIELEN (ME) to turn, wheel. Forms: WHIELYNG, *pres. pt.*

WHIST (ME) quiet.

WIDLAND (OE) wide region. Forms:—, *ac. pl.*

WIELL (OE) wellspring. Forms: WIELLE. *dat. sing.*

WIELLSPRYNG (OE) fountain, spring. Forms: WIELL-
      SPRYNGES, *gen. sing.*

WIJF (ME) wife.

WILDE (OE) untamed, wild. Forms:—, *neut. ac. sing.*

WILFULLYE (ME) willingly.

WILLEN (ME) to will, wish. Forms: WILT, *2 pres. sing.*;
      WOLEN, *3 pres. pl.*; WOLDE, *3 p. sing.*; WOLDEN,
      3 p. pl.

WILNIAN (OE) to desire. Forms: WILNIAÞ, *pres. pl.*

WINNEN (ME) to win. Forms: WONNEN, *p. pt.*

WINTERĊEALD (OE) winter's cold. Forms: WINTER-
      ĊEALDE, *dat. sing.*

WINTER-TID (OE) winter time.

WIS (OE) sensible, wise.

WISA (OE) leader.

WISCH (Obs.) to wish. Forms: WISCHETH, *3 pres. sing.*

WITA (OE) wise man. Forms: WITAN, *ac. pl.*

WIT(E) (ME) to know. Forms: WOOT, *3 pres. sing.*

WIÞDRAWEN (ME) to withdraw. Forms: WIÞDRAWEÞ, *3 pres. sing.*; WIÞDRAWE, *p. pt.*

WIÞERWEARD (OE) adverse, contending. Forms: WIÞER-WEARDE, *fem. nom. pl.*

WIÞHOLDEN (ME) to restrain.

WIÞOUTEFORÞE (ME) from outside.

WIÞSTONDAN (OE) to resist, withstand. Forms: WIÞSTONDAÞ, *3 pres. pl.*

WI(Þ)(TH)(-)YNNE (ME) within.

WLITE (OE) appearance, form.

WOD (OE) crazy, mad.

WODNES (OE) madness. Forms: WODNESSE, *ac. sing.*

WOFULL (ME) woeful.

WOLCEN (OE) cloud. Forms: WOLCNU, *ac. pl.*; WOLCNUM, *dat. pl.*

WOLD (Obs.) would.

WON (Obs.) conquered.

WONDAR (Obs.) wonder.

WONDREN (ME) to be amazed, wonder. Forms: WON-DREÞ, *3 pres. sing.*

WOOD(E) (ME) crazy, mad.

WOODEN (ME) to rage. Forms:—, *3 pres. pl.*

WORLD(E) (ME) earth, world. Forms: WORLDES, *gen. sing.*

WORÞ (ME) value, worth.

WORULD (OE) world. Forms: WORULDE, *ac. sing.*

WORULDSĊEAT (OE) region. Forms: WORULDSĊEATAS, *ac. pl.*; WORULDSCEATE, *dat. sing.*

WOUNDE (ME) injury, wound.

WRAÞÞ(E) (ME) anger. Forms: WRAÞÞES, *pl.*

WRAWE (ME, Obs.) angry, fearsome.

WREĊĊA (OE) exile. Forms: WREĊĊAN, *nom. pl.*

WRECCHE (ME) wretch. Forms: WRECCHES, *pl.*

WRECCHED(E) (ME) wretched.

WRECEND (OE) avenger.

WRENĊAN (OE) to turn, twist. Forms: WRENĊEÞ, *3 pres. sing.*

WREÞIAN (OE) to support, sustain. Forms: WREÞAÞ, *3 pres. sing.*

WRIÞAN (OE) to bind, tie. Forms: WRIÞÞ, *3 pres. sing.*

WRITBOC (OE) writing tablet. Forms: WRITBEC, *gen. sing.*

WROTHE (Obs.) wrath.

WRY (Obs.) to turn away, bend, twist. Forms: WRIES, *3 pres. sing.*; WRYING, *pres. pt.*

WULDOR (OE) glory.

WULF (OE) wolf. Forms: WULFUM, *dat. pl.*

WUNDORLEOHT (OE) wonderful light.

WUNDRIAN (OE) to wonder at. Forms: WUNDRAÞ, *3 pres. sing.*

WYL (Obs.) will.

WYRD (OE) fate. Forms:—, *ac. sing.*

WYRTCRÆFTIĠ (OE) skilled in herbs. Forms: WYRT-
    CRÆFTIĠAN, *fem. nom. sing.*

YDEL (ME) empty. Phrases: IN YDEL, in vain.

YEE (ME) yea.

YEE (Obs.) eye. Forms: YEES, *pl.*

YEER (ME) year. Forms: YERES, *pl.*

YELDEN (ME) to give, repay, yield. Forms: YELDEÞ, *3 pres.
    sing.;* YELD, *3 p. sing.*

YEME (ME) to heed. Forms: YEMEÞ, *3 pres. sing.*

YEVEN (ME) to give. Forms: YAF, *3 pres. sing.;* YYVE, *pres.
    subj. pl.;* YYVEN, *p. pt.*

YFEL (OE) evil, wickedness. Forms: YF(E)LUM, *dat. pl.*

YIF (ME) if.

YIFT (ME) gift.

YIT (ME) yet.

YLORN (ME) lost.

YMAGE (ME) image, impression. Forms: YMAGES, *pl.*

YMBWINDAN (OE) to enfold. Forms: YMBWINDEÞ, *3
    pres. sing.*

YNNE (ME) in.

YNNERE (ME) inner, inward.

YNOUGH (Obs.) enough.

YOK (ME) yoke.

YOURE (ME) your.

YOW (ME) you.

YRE (Obs.) anger, ire.

YÞ (OE) wave. Forms: YÞA, *ac. pl.*

ZEPHYRUS (L) the west wind.